VISUAL ARTS
●f the
liquid packaging

Design Media Publishing Limited

Contents

Preface

At the beginning of the twentieth century, people would go to the grocery store near their home to buy their oil to cook. They would come with an empty bottle, and the grocer, whom they knew for a long time, would fill it from a large tank.

Then came the time of the competition and the "hyper choice". More and more brands, belonging to more and more groups, were proposing the same products to the consumer. To lead the consumer on the difficult road of choice, marketing teams and designers began to create product personalities, to create advertising to explain them and, of course, to design the brands, the labels, the bottles, to express these peculiarities. The consumer became the happy chooser.

In 2011 was published a fascinating study by Sheena Lyengar, a professor at the Columbia Business School, called "The Art of Choosing". The incredible conclusion of this study is that the so-called great progress of our contemporary time, the "hyper choice" does not generate the happiness of the consumer. On the contrary, many times, too much choice puts the consumer in a doubt, what I would call a "shelf fog", which leads to an impossibility to choose.

In other words, the choice, instead of pushing the sales, would decrease them? What is the vision of packaging designers in this new world? I believe

- this is time to create products with integrity and respect of the consumer.

-

- This is time to create products with real personalities, a strong style, and no
- more "me too", which take useless shelf space.

-

- This is time to break all codes, break all rules; this is the time for inventing,
- with only one goal:

-

- Only use our design talents to create great, unique products that will meet the
- client profound desires.

-

- If we cannot do that, we should wait, and not participate to fill the shelves
- uselessly!

Elie Papiernik
Co-founder, and Design Director
Centdegrés
France

DRY Soda

The designers first designed DRY Soda's packaging when the company launched in 2005. Since that time DRY has evolved from its beginnings on the white tablecloths of the country's finest restaurants, to finding huge success in grocery stores, cafés, and other retail locations across the US and Canada. In response to these changing markets and retail conditions, DRY Soda asked the designers to evolve their packaging. Bold, graphic illustrations stand out at retail and characterise DRY's distinctive flavours and its uniqueness as an all natural soda. Clear bottles allow the purity of the product to show through and the founder's signature on each bottle connotes a sense of craft behind each flavour's recipe.

Design Agency: *Turnstyle*. Production Date: *2010*. Creative Director: *Steven Watson*. Designer: *Steven Watson*. Client: *DRY Soda Company*. Nationality: *USA*.

Fizzy Lizzy

Identity and packaging redesign for a line of all-natural, carbonated fruit juice beverages. A bold and refreshing drink without the typical added sugars and other junk, the design neatly tells the whole story: bubbles and fruit are all you need.

Design Agency: *JJAAKK*. Production Date: *2010*. Creative Director:*Jesse Kirsch*. Art Director:*Jesse Kirsch*. Designer: *Jesse Kirsch*. Client: *Fizzy Lizzy*. Nationality: *USA*.

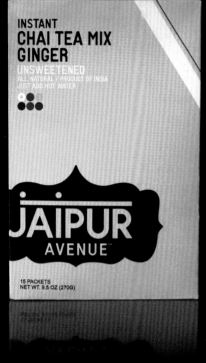

INSTANT
**CHAI TEA MIX
GINGER**
UNSWEETENED
ALL NATURAL / PRODUCT OF INDIA
JUST ADD HOT WATER

15 PACKETS
NET WT. 9.5 OZ (270G)

The faraway Indian city of Jaipur, famous for its royal palaces, colourful culture and romantic charm epitomises the ancient chai tradition at its best. In the packaging and brand identity for this line of chai tea products, the designers set out to evoke this enthralling, magical locale through a modern reinterpretation of its diverse colour palette and icon motifs.

Design Agency: *Turnstyle*. Production Date: *2010*. Creative Director: *Ben Graham*. Designer: *Madeleine Eiche*. Client: *Jaipur Avenue*. Nationality: *USA*.

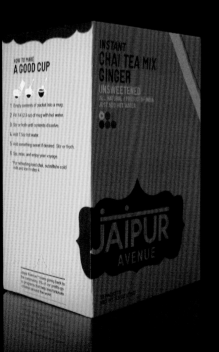

INSTANT
**CHAI TEA MIX
VARIETY PACK**
UNSWEETENED
ALL NATURAL / PRODUCT OF INDIA
JUST ADD HOT WATER

JAIPUR
AVENUE™

20 PACKETS
NET WT. 9.8 OZ (280G)

INSTANT
**CHAI TEA MIX
VANILLA**
UNSWEETENED
ALL NATURAL / PRODUCT OF INDIA
JUST ADD HOT WATER

JAIPUR
AVENUE™

20 PACKETS
NET WT. 9.8 OZ (280G)

INSTANT
**CHAI TEA MIX
GINGER**
UNSWEETENED
ALL NATURAL / PRODUCT OF INDIA
JUST ADD HOT WATER

JAIPUR
AVENUE™

15 PACKETS
NET WT. 9.5 OZ (270G)

INSTANT
**CHAI TEA MIX
ORIGINAL
MASALA**
UNSWEETENED
ALL NATURAL / PRODUCT OF INDIA
JUST ADD HOT WATER

JAIPUR
AVENUE™

20 PACKETS
NET WT. 9.8 OZ (280G)

INSTANT
**CHAI TEA MIX
CARDAMOM**
UNSWEETENED
ALL NATURAL / PRODUCT OF INDIA
JUST ADD HOT WATER

JAIPUR
AVENUE™

20 PACKETS
NET WT. 9.8 OZ (280G)

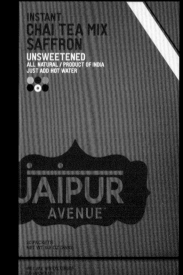

INSTANT
**CHAI TEA MIX
SAFFRON**
UNSWEETENED
ALL NATURAL / PRODUCT OF INDIA
JUST ADD HOT WATER

JAIPUR
AVENUE™

20 PACKETS
NET WT. 9.8 OZ (280G)

Coca-cola 2007 Holiday Cans

The designers couldn't have been more excited when what is perhaps the most recognised brand in the world, Coca-Cola, called them. The initial assignment was to create packaging for the relaunch of Coca-Cola Vanilla, a product that had been off market for several years. Coca-Cola then returned to Hatch for help with their Holiday 2007 campaign, "Give, Live, Love." For the holiday campaign, the designers created a series of unique graphic illustrations, each representing hallmark characteristics of the company's five leading brands: Coca-Cola Classic, Diet Coke, Coca-Cola Zero, Sprite, and Fanta. In each of the collaborations with Coca-Cola, the challenge was to find the right visual and emotive balance between the brand iconography and goals of the campaign – whether it was refreshing brand attributes, creating new packaging or integrating a seasonal element into the existing brand.

Design Agency: *Hatch Design*. Production Date: *2007*. Creative Director: *Katie Jain / Joel Templin*. Designer: *Ryan Meis*. Client: *The Coca–Cola Company*. Nationality: *USA*.

⟁ Charitea

The drinks market is extremely competitive and it is hard for new products to come on the market and be seen, which makes the packaging especially important in this category. The design should draw attention to it and simultaneously be unique and "iconic", timeless and modern. It should signal good quality but not premium and luxury. Simultaneously the design should effectively challenge the conceptions of how "charity products" and organic products should look. The product should be in demand and bought by everyone, not only those who actively look for organic goods or normal consumers who buy on impulse because of a bad conscience. Charitea's totally white symbol – a tea leaf or a drop – hovers harmonically over the logo. Elegant, but eye-catching. The products included in the series of freshly-brewed organic teas are distinguished through their simple name: Charitea black, Charitea red and Charitea green, that of course refer to the different types of tea. Charitea is designed for the health conscious and socially committed consumer. A drink with a conscience. A good drink!

Design Agency: *BVD*. Production Date: *2009*. Designer: *Susanna Nygren Barrett / Kina Giesenfeld / Bengt Anderung*. Client: *Lemonaid GmbH*. Nationality: *Sweden*.

Tesco Green and Herbal Teas

The key selling point was the flavour of the tea so the focus of the design was to create a fruit or herb story with photography being used to establish each flavour variant. A drawstring tea bag was used for the descriptor holding device. Once the design had been selected, Tesco management decided to increase the range from 3 products to 10. The range was launched in May 2009.

Design Agency: *R Design*. Production Date: *2009*. Creative Director: *Dave Richmond*. Designer: *Gareth Roberts*. Client: *Tesco*. Nationality: *UK*.

Arla Milk Bottle

Pucko is a classic chocolate drink brand in Sweden with an iconic glass bottle. Arla Foods wanted to refine the brand identity that it would work on additional packaging types and sizes.

A complete identity system that was successfully applied to new packaging types without losing the original look and feel of the brand.

Considerable increase in sales indicating a successful transfer into new packaging types.

Design Agency: *Neumeister Strategic Design AB.*
Production Date: *2008.* Designer: *Peter Neumeister / Mattias Lindstedt.* Client: *Pucko.* Nationality: *Sweden.*

 **First Blush**

First Blush is a juice that Ferroconcrete has transformed into something much more grown up. Recognising the juice itself as the soul of the brand, Ferroconcrete allowed it to shine through the elegant glass bottles. The brand conveys that this juice is fresh-picked, healthy and truly sophisticated.

Design Agency: *Ferroconcrete*. Production Date: *2008*. Creative Director: *Yolanda Santosa*. Designer: *Yolanda Santosa / Sunjoo Park / Wendy Thai / Ann Kim*. Client: *First Blush Inc.* Photography: *Paul Taylor*. Nationality: *USA*.

Lass–Made With Joy

Made with Joy is a new kind of food and beverage company. They have recently launched their new range of Lassi drinks with the help of the House London. The House helped choose the name, create the identity, produce the packaging and launch the new website. The design is based on Indian colours, bling and patterns. A bold design that is already proving a hit in the shops of London town.

Design Agency: *The House London Ltd.* Production Date: *2010–2011.* Creative Director: *Michael Murdoch.* Designer: *Elsie Wong.* Client: *Made With Joy Foods Ltd.* Photography: *Mowie Kay.* Nationality: *UK.*

Ping Energy Drink

Demonstrate an advanced investigation and research into an area of interest and "inspiration" revolving around some form of design communication and produce an identity for your chosen matter.

The designer decided to look into the harmful consumption of energy drinks and how they are becoming more are more popular in our busy society.

In response, he created a healthy energy drink called Ping which can still bring you that "energy high" but without the dirty chemicals and high amounts of sugar. All the contents have been labelled on the front in the shape of a speedometer.

Production Date: *2010*. Designer: *Anne Dahlin*. Client: *Anne Dahlin*. Nationality: *Sweden*.

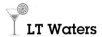

LT Waters

The designers were commissioned by a company located in St. Tropez. Les Tropeziennes is a registered trademark and there are several products under that name. The brand owner asked the designers to design a line of refreshing water flavours with three variants, Beach, Sport and Night.

They have made the project with a big load of sensuality and novelty and the pyramidal shape is determined without adhesive labels, all information held in screen printing and relief for the brand.

It is a young, feminine, sensual and innovative packaging highly adapted to their origin, St. Tropez.

Design Agency: *Corretje Comunicación Grafica.* Production Date: *2010.* Designer: *Xavier Corretje / Ana Hernando.* Client: *LT Waters.* Nationality: *Spain.*

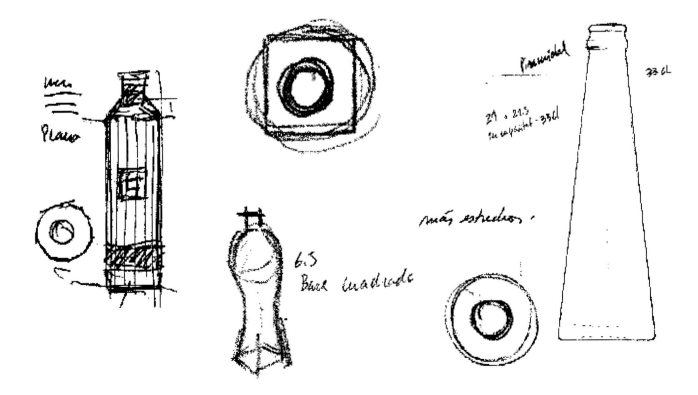

U Hydration Packaging

Nuun is the leading manufacturer of electrolyte sports drink tablets. After establishing a strong reputation with endurance athletes, the company hired Moxie Sozo to launch a new product targeting the health-conscious women's lifestyle market. The agency, through research and focus groups, identified competitive challenges and opportunities for the new brand. Using a graphic architecture centred around a dynamic female form, contemporary styling and a fresh colour scheme, "U" capitalised on key emotional drivers of the target audience, while maintaining taste appeal and a strong shelf presence. The packaging has won several awards, been featured in numerous books and received praise for its effectiveness.

Design Agency: *Moxie Sozo.* Production Date: *2008.* Creative Director: *Leif Steiner.* Designer: *Charles Bloom / Stephanie Shank.* Client: *Nuun.* Nationality: *USA.*

natural
hydration™

GOJI BERRY
GREEN TEA

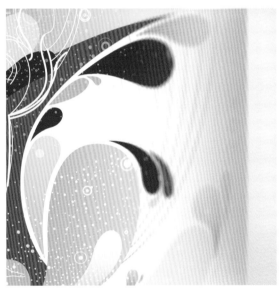

natural
hydration

TANGERINE

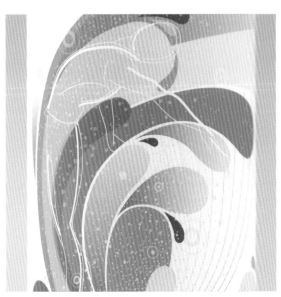

natural
hydration™

LEMON
CHAI

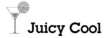

Juicy Cool

Juicy Cool drinks with unusual and uncommon fruit tastes, based on natural fruit juice. The brand is for the young and wild, searching for something new and unusual, those that are not interested in traditional juices and cold teas. The primary goal of the project was to create a new image, corresponding to the bright and extreme character of the brand and the expectations of the target audience - active, progressive part of the youth.

Design Agency: *KIAN Brand Agency.* Production Date: *2009.* Creative Director: *Kirill Konstantinov.* Designer: *Irina Goosevskaya.* Client: *Raimbek Bottlers CO (Kazakhstan).* Nationality: *Russia.*

Tango

Blue Marlin created a new identity that is modern, fresh, fun, impactful and most of all a clear expression of the brand's innate nature. Where many brands have been using fruit imagery in a cute, innocent way, Tango's packaging shows it like it is with fruit getting crushed, punctured, mangled, mauled and mashed up. The graphics are striking and humorous, while graffiti style type and illustrations give the brand a little edge without taking itself too seriously. Little lines of copy complete the look and feel with deadpan delivery suited to Tango's values. When Tango is in the hands of its target audience its brand values of impact and entertainment come across loud and clear.

The challenge was to make the most of Tango's unique personality and full taste to drive value share growth. The strategy of previous years had been to appease the gatekeepers – mothers – and Tango's personality and attitude had been deliberately dialled down in packaging and advertising. Blue Marlin recognised that in today's market conditions Tango's greatest asset lay in its distinctive humorous personality. The task was to recapture Tango's irreverent sense of fun and full on taste in a new brand identity, packaging, tone of voice and off pack communications.

Design Agency: *Blue Marlin*. Production Date: *2009*. Client: *Britvic Soft Drinks*. Photography: *Blue Marlin*. Nationality: *UK*.

Fruit Invaders Design

Vivaks, a well - known Macedonian juice producer, decided to make their brand more relevant to a younger, urban & more contemporary target. How to do it best? By launching a special pack edition of their existing product line Viva. And here it is, the first line of special pack edition Fruit Invaders. Let's keep our thumbs up and hope for many new special editions!

Design Agency: *New Moment–New Ideas Company Y&R Skopjeproduction*. Production Date: *2011*. Designer: *Nikola Vojnov*. Client: *Vivaks*. Nationality: *Macedon.*

Quick Fruit
Packaging Concept

The idea behind Quick Fruit packaging is a fruit sliced in half showing the core of the fruit as the lid of the product. A clean, simple logo with the letter "Q" depicting a cup with a spoon appears on the lid and side.

Design Agency: *Circum Punkt Design*. Production Date: *2008*. Designer: *Marcel Buerkle*. Nationality: *South Africa*.

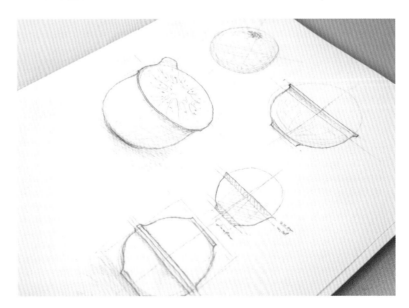

Angelini Design took irony and self-referentiality as their guidelines when restyling Aranciosa, Limoncedro and Gassosa Neri. Labels that evoke a glorious past and carry a historic tradition into the future: the transparent material gives every label the colour of the original product, contained in an uneven, vintage style bottle.

Design Agency: *Angelini Design*. Production Date: *2007*. Client: *Chin8 Neri*. Nationality: *Italy*.

Grove Organic Fruit Co.

Grove's unique selling point of "organic" no longer had the cut through required for the brand to distinguish it as "The Original". The designers created an illustrated design that brought to life the premium preposition of this independent brand- the bold citrus on black identity grows into a grove of fruit when packs are merchandised side-by-side supermarket shelf, reinforcing the brand name. The redesign has cemented Grove as the England's number one best selling organic juice brand.

Design Agency: *BrandOpus*. Production Date: *2010*. Creative Director: *Paul Taylor*.
Client: *Wellness Foods*. Nationality: *UK*.

Drink Local

Local is an identity the designer created for an organic drink based around it being part of the locavore movement, meaning that all the ingredients are all grown and produced locally to where it is bottled and sold. The logo is a combination of three elements: a location marker to represent the locavore movement, a speech bubble because of the activism involved, and a water droplet. The designer designed four different flavours and created a label for each using maps and a cityscape as design elements. The cap of the bottle says local, and the hole for it in the carrier has the logo mark. So when there is a drink in the carrier and it is viewed from the top it recreates the logo.

Production Date: *2007*. Creative Director: *Ben Langholz*. Designer: *Ben Langholz*. Client: *Academy of Art University*. Photography: *Ben Langholz*. Nationality: *USA*.

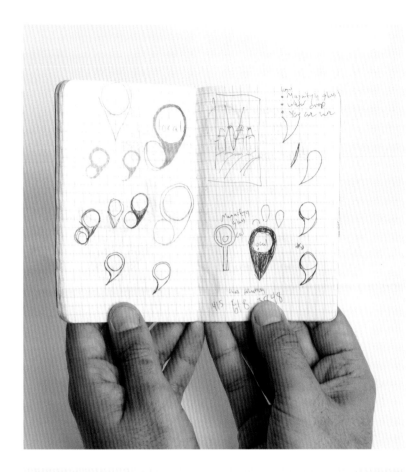

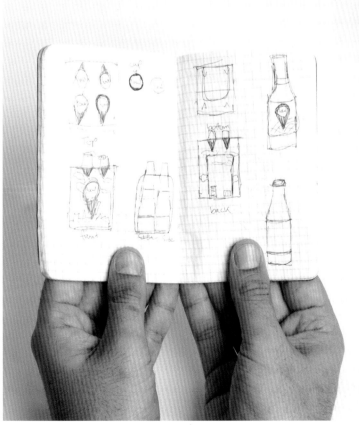

 COCO

Coco carried with it a considerable volume of information that had to be communicated in terms that consumers would readily understand. There was a great deal that needed to be explained, from what coco juice is and its many benefits to the unique process by which it was extracted. The information also had to be set in a way that did not overpower the design of the pack.

The copy explaining Dr Martins' Coco water, juice and cream were keys to meeting the lengthy brief, so Blue Marlin made sure that the pack design could hold ample text in an aesthetically pleasing way. They developed an amusingly literal tone of voice that engaged consumers and conveyed the doctor's obsessive approach to his products. The pack copy set the direction for the brand's marketing communications with the "shh!" strategy that debuted on pack subsequently being applied to Public relation and in-store advertising.

Design Agency: *Blue Marlin*. Production Date: *2007*. Client: *Dr Antonio Martins*. Photography: *Blue Marlin*. Nationality: *USA*.

Mood Energy Drink

The brand Mood emerged from a desire of AmPm Brazil to launch his own brand of beverages, starting with energy drinks. Rather than giving the same name for the brand, the designers proposed to create a stronger brand concept, which could better connect with the audience. Under the concept of "positive energy" they named it "mood", a brand focused on products for an active lifestyle, which are able to bring more energy and optimism to people's lives. The logo shows that these two aspects are within the mark. The packaging look is intended to challenge the category visual codes by abusing the white colour and clear style, and suggest the consumption of the product out of the nightlife. The colours refer to colours of the brand AmPm. The brand has redefined the concept of private label at AmPm, accounting for 30% of the energy drink sales in less than a year. The brand is now preparing its expansion to other types of beverages.

Design Agency: *Fabio Seva Design*. Production Date: *2010*. Creative Director: *Fabio Seva*. Designer: *Fabio Seva*. Client: *E+BROS Brand & Product Developers in association to AmPm*. Photography: *Fabio Seva*. Nationality: *Brazil*.

Anheuser–Busch Inbev

Deutsch Design Works has developed multiple brand innovations including over 10 unique brand applications of aluminium "bottlecans" for Anheuser-Busch brands. One note of distinction, the flaming eagle design was targeted to increasing brand awareness with nationwide motorcycle events.

Design Agency: *Deutsch Design Works*. Production Date: *2006–2009*. Art Director: *Barry Deutsch*. Client: *Anheuser–Busch InBev*. Nationality: *USA*.

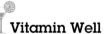

Vitamin Well

Vitamin Well was launched as "the tasty, healthy drink filled with minerals". Its success was far greater than anyone could imagine. But was the existing design sufficiently clear? Neumeister were contracted to add an even greater clarity to the design and give the brand a new lease of life.

The design was revamped and developed. The labelling and the packaging – everything got a new clear structure, which nevertheless kept the original idea clearly in focus. The designers gave Vitamin Well the very vitamin injections that it gives you.

The bottle alone conveys the message in all the advertising. No copy, no other visual impressions. A great success has become even greater.

Design Agency: *Neumeister Strategic Design AB*. Production Date: *2008*. Creative Director: *Peter Neumeister*. Designer: *Peter Neumeister / Tobias Andersson*. Client: *Vitamin Well*. Nationality: *Sweden*.

Cidriya Premium Cider

The clear but sharp detailed design for this cider reflects the core of this product: the product itself. Made from 100% pink lady apples grown in the high mountains of Northern Israel, the design accents the product, hinting details of the delicate and precise process of creating this premium, crisp cider. The Hebrew typography and metallic foils create a visually stimulating product while not taking focus off of the product itself.

Design Agency: *Kroll.* Production Date: *2011.* Creative Director: *Dov Kroll.* Designer: *Dov Kroll.* Photography: *Yasmin & Arye–Studio Ya.* Nationality: *Israel.*

POW Energy Drink

POW Energy Drink is a fruit - based energy drink aimed at young vibrant out going people. Made from natural fruit juices it can be enjoyed as a pick - me - up drink in the morning or can be mixed with vodka to make an uplifting cocktail on a night out. The design approach was to come up with a strong, bold identity and packaging to match the vibrant nature of the brand and stand out in a very competitive market place. One of the key elements that separate POW Energy Drink from the competition is the flavours. The main aim was to clearly illustrate the fruit element without making it seem like just a fruit drink. Using the natural colours of the fruits used in the drink the designers created a very strong and bold colour palette which was applied to the packaging.

Design Agency: *Siaw Misa*. Production Date: *2010*. Creative Director: *Abuakwa Siaw–Misa*. Designer: *Abuakwa Siaw–Misa*. Client: *Pow Energy Drink Ltd.* Photography: *Theodore Alexander*. Nationality: *UK*.

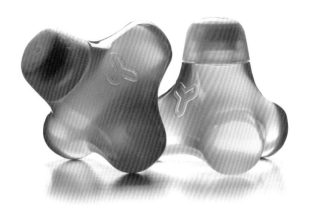

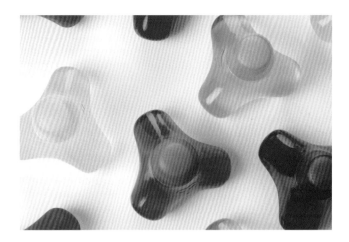

Y Water

To create an entirely new product and brand from the ground up, including everything from the iconic "tetra pod" shaped bottle and "Y Knots" (rubber connectors that let kids connect and build with the bottles) to the logo, brand identity and messaging.

Y Water is a unique tetra-pod shape that eliminates the need for extra branding by placing all required language on a biodegradable tag that doubles as a merchandising hook.

Design Agency: *Fuse Design*. Production Date: *2008*. Client: *Y Water*. Nationality: *USA*.

 Mixed

The idea of this project is to sell emotions through a product. The designer selected a mix between a concoction and vodka. The concoction is a fruit blend that contains emotions such as love, sadness, happiness, fear and anger. The Mixed Emotions cocktail evokes an emotion and changes your attitude according to your preference. The spiral structure forms two straws that invite the consumer to visualise how the liquids combine as they drink. Two tiny mechanisms outline the straws to bottom of the container, allowing air to enter and hence permitting the customer to absorb the liquid. The cap provides an air-tight seal, thus enclosing all openings.

While the front panel invites the consumer to drink, the back panel depicts phrases to illustrate the type of experience the customer will encounter. Because of its design, the consumers can dance, jump, go wild or do whatever they please without worrying about spilling their drink or breaking the bottle.

Design Agency: *Gworkshop*. Production Date: *2009*. Creative Director: *José Luis García Eguiguren*. Designer: *José Luis García Eguiguren*. Client: *Mixed Emotions*. Nationality: *Ecuador*.

▼ Wildberry Cooler

Ultra trendy, super stylish and dramatically different, this update unabashedly declares "girls night out". The sensual allure of this design is immediately recognisable on shelf and stands out against competitors in this cluttered category. The brand identity is shortened to "Wild" to accommodate additional flavours.

Design Agency: *Davis*. Production Date: *2010*. Designer: *Jeff Boulton*. Account Director: *Jeff Davis*. Client: *Corby Distilleries*. Nationality: *Canada*.

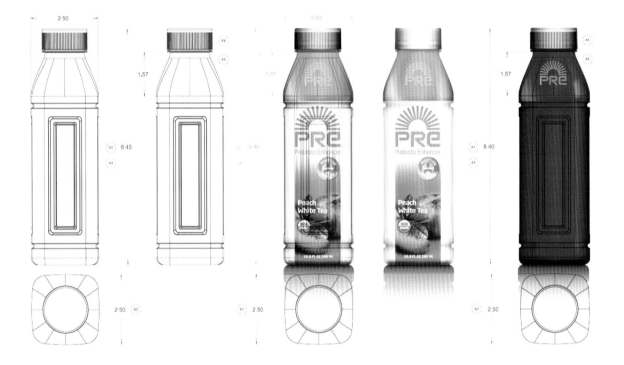

PRE–Branding and Packaging

Experience a new kind of beverage, PRE Probiotic Enhancer, an amazingly delicious fusion of organic juice enhanced with a proprietary prebiotic blend developed by Jarrow Formulas. PRE prebiotic beverage was developed to conveniently deliver you a healthy digestive boost any time of the day. PRE actively works with the body to promote healthy digestive balance by triggering the growth of beneficial bacteria called probiotics already present in your digestive tract. As the good bacteria increase so does resistance to harmful bacteria causing a boost in your immune system. PRE works with your digetive system helping to restore balance creating a healthy, happier you.

Design Agency: *TomTor Studio*. Production Date: *2009*. Creative Director: *Tom Tor*. Designer: *Tom Tor*. Client: *Pre*. Photography: *Tom Tor*. Nationality: *USA*.

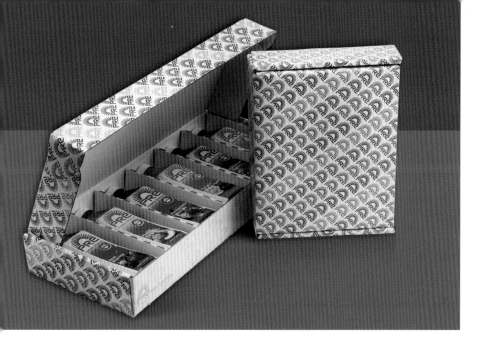

JUS

Jus packaging is as fresh and delicious as the juice within. This playful bottle is functional, delightful, and innovative.

Design Agency: *Karim Rashid Inc.* Production Date: *2010.* Nationality: *USA.*

 EAU

Clean, contemporary, and organic, Karim's design for EAU, by Paris Baguette offers
fluid beauty, while staying simple and modern.

Design Agency: *Karim Rashid Inc.* Production Date: *2010.* Nationality: *USA.*

Gorobel Premium Basque Water

Packaging for the first mineral basque water named Gorobel. Gorobel is the Basque name of the Sierra de la Salvada, a landmark between Vizcaya, Alava and Burgos 'hidden' one of the largest and richest reserves of flora and fauna in Europe. One of its springs starts in Gorobel, the first premium water from the Basque Country, rich in minerals and purity levels similar to those of spring water at a much higher altitude.

Design Agency: *Isusko.* Production Date: *2011.* Creative Director: *Isusko Artabe.* Designer: *Isusko Artabe.* Client: *JGG.* Photography: *Isusko Artabe.* Nationality: *Spain.*

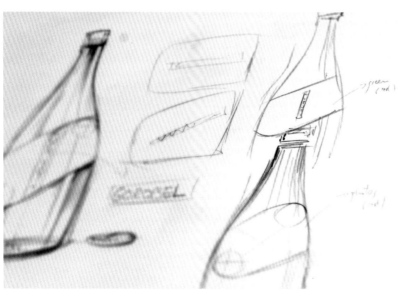

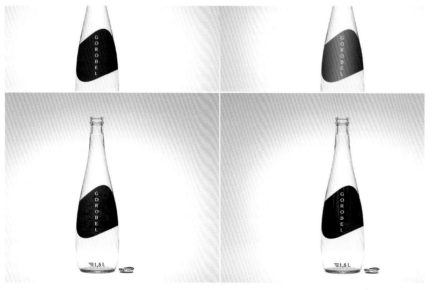

Schweppes Limited Edition Range

The Limited Edition range is a selection of 300mL Schweppes Classic Mixers that celebrate the enigmatic and innovative spirit of this beautiful and iconic brand. Each image, originally from the Schweppes poster art archive, was respectfully retouched and adjusted to express the unique personality of the individual product.

Design Agency: *DiDONATO Partners*. Production Date: *2010*. Creative Director: *Damian Kelly*. Designer: *Damian Kelly*. Client: *Schweppes Australia*. Photography: *Schweppes Archive / DiDONATO*. Nationality: *Australia*.

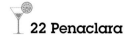

22 Penaclara

Name and packaging design for the launch of 22°C Premium Water aimed at hotel and specialised store sectors. A simple and direct typographical design which the absence of colour is prized. The origin of the name is directly related to the temperature of the water in the source spring, 22°C.

Design Agency: *(calcco) Comunicación Visual.* Production Date: *2009.* Creative Director: *Sergio Aja.* Designer: *Eduardo del Pozo.* Client: *MINERAQUA, S.A.* Photography: *Sergio Aja.* Nationality: *Spain.*

Echo

What makes echo stand out from other bottled waters is its simplicity; it is bottled water that minimises its environmental impact. Clean, modern and responsible – the design of the packaging keeps waste to an absolute minimum. Even the quick-peel removable labels were also printed in a carbon neutral, wind-powered facility.

Design Agency: *Ferroconcrete*. Production Date: *2010*. Creative Director: *Yolanda Santosa*. Designer: *Yolanda Santosa / Owen Gee*. Client: *Echo Beverages*. Nationality: *USA*.

Kacheli

During the process of working on the project, several options were suggested to create a positive brand conception and strong brand identity. The first option suggests pulling the attention towards the natural products used in the making. This idea is supported by an eco-friendly, refined design, assuming the presence of a bright visual brand identity. The second option is oriented towards more progressive and modern target audience and involves an innovative minimal design, concurrent with the latest European trends. The third option appeals to the traditional values. The developed conception suggests a calm but colourful solution, using engraving technology in the formation of the background, as well as an extensive area for client communication, used to deliver all the advantages of the product to the consumer via the label.

Design Agency: *KIAN Brand Agency*. Production Date: *2010*. Creative Director: *Kirill Konstantinov*. Designer: *Andrey Kalashnikov*. Client: *Raimbek Bottlers CO (Kazakhstan)*. Nationality: *Russia*.

Isst Organic Ice Tea

ARTENTIKO developed complete branding for a new line of beverages.

Due to an increased competition in the beverage market of the "ice tea" type, the designers were to redefine the concept and prepare the visual concept of flavoured organic beverages based on tea, both light and refreshing. The brand was to offer not only the drink, refreshment and original flavour, but also a style which could become part of a lifestyle. ARTENTIKO prepared a complete branding strategy and graphic solution including: brand name, architecture, flavours, colours, packaging, advertising slogans, billboards & posters, promo-cars, website.

Design Agency: *ARTENTIKO*. Production Date: *2010*. Creative Director: *Marcin Kaczmarek*. Designer: *Marcin Kaczmarek*. Nationality: *Poland*.

☒ Hampstead Tea

Create a range of packaging that reflected the organic/biodynamic purity of the
single estate and herbal leaf teas. It's designed for 25 to 45 - year - old discerning
tea drinkers. An image of natural purity—tea infusing in pure clear water. A pack
design that set new rules in the speciality tea sector. Design simplicity and elegant
photography give a clarity of message for this range of luxury organic teas.

Design Agency: *Mayday (London)*. Production Date: *2006*. Creative Director: *Barry
Gillibrand*. Designer: *Roger Akroyd*. Client: *Hampstead Tea London*. Photography:
Andy Seymour / Jonathon Knowles. Nationality: *UK*.

Cuculand

Identity and packaging design for a brand addressing those who are young, pure &
free. Cuculand ("cuckooland") is the imaginary life in a real country, or the other way
around, as illustrated with humour on the Ice Tea packages. Eventually, we all live in
Cuculand.

Design Agency: *Brandient.* Production Date: *2009.* Creative Director: *Cristian 'Kit'
Paul.* Designer: *Cristian Petre / Cristian 'Kit' Paul / Bogdan Dumitrache / Ciprian
Badalan.* Client: *Trigento Marketing.* Nationality: *Romania.*

Zoega

Zoega, a dark-roasted coffee favourite in Sweden, is expanding to the rest of Scandinavia. A stringent design and name concept had to be established - one that could stand the test of time.

The Z is vital to Zoega - a dark - roasted coffee that tastes more. All product names include a Z, together with a taste description, and a design solution that shows a potent product without any unnecessary fuss. Out now in Denmark and Norway.

Design Agency: *Neumeister Strategic Design AB.* Production Date: *2010.* Creative Director: *Peter Neumeister.* Designer: *Peter Neumeister / Tobias Andersson.* Client: *Nestle Norden.* Nationality: *Switzerland.*

Starbucks Doubleshot Grande

Who better to offer caffeinated energy drinks than the company that sells more coffee drinks than anyone? When Starbucks decided to develop three flavours to be sold in both their own stores and in other less controlled, more crowded venues, they asked Hatch for help. That in itself is noteworthy. Starbucks rarely collaborates with designers outside its corporate walls, but openly pulled Hatch into the process. The drink concept and name changed over many months, and the designers partnered with Starbucks to give visual expression to various concepts throughout the six-month development phase. Ultimately, they decided on offering three flavours under the name Starbucks Doubleshot Grande.

Design Agency: *Hatch Design*. Production Date: *2008*. Creative Director: *Katie Jain / Joel Templin*. Designer: *Ryan Meis*. Client: *Starbucks Coffee Company*. Nationality: *USA*.

⚕ Friele Iced Coffee–Frozen Aroma

In 2010 Friele launched a new, iced coffee range, and the task was to create a sub
brand and strategy to target a younger audience.

The designers created a simple, strong sub - brand - Friele IS (ice). Rich colours
were used to convey depth of flavour, using the metal nature of the can substrate
to give a subtle sparkle and the IS illustration was created to show the ice growing
organically from the letters.

Design Agency: *YOU*. Production Date: *2010*. Designer: *Robyn Stevenson / Jeremy
Chestnutt / Esme Fisher / David Muzeen / Ninja Scheel Aas / Jackie Hall / Candy
Schneider / Ian Burren / Stephen Elliott*. Client: *Kaffehuset Friele*. Nationality:
Norway.

Tau Delta Gourmet Foods

Tau Delta gourmet foods entered the gourmet market with a richly stylised package. Tridimage's brief was to convey Tau Delta's core brand values of quality and natural ingredients. As the category was flooded with crafty, homemade-looking products, Tridimage decided to try a more refined approach in order to stand out. White and a different colour coding each variety compose the spine of the resulting design, aiming for an elegant yet tempting subtle feeling.

Design Agency: *Tridimage*. Production Date: *2009*. Creative Director: *Adriana Cortese / Virginia Gines / Hernán Braberman*. Client: *Tau Delta*. Photography: *Dany Kamida*. Nationality: *Argentina*.

 Maison Orphée

Develop new packaging for Maison Orphée, a producer and importer of oils and condiments. The packaging strategy is based on the insight that consumers increasingly distinguish between everyday cooking products and gourmet serving products. The Cooking line, which features oils and condiments, is shown here.

Design Agency: *lg2boutique*. Production Date: *2010*. Creative Director: *Claude Auchu*. Designer: *Serge Côté*. Nationality: *Canada*.

MAISON ORPHÉE

POUR LES VINAIGRETTES... ET PLUS
FOR VINAIGRETTES... AND MORE

BIOLOGIQUE ❧ ORGANIC

Moutarde *de Dijon*
Dijon Mustard
250 ml

MAISON ORPHÉE

POUR LES MARINADES... ET PLUS
FOR MARINADES... AND MORE

BIOLOGIQUE ❧ ORGANIC

Moutarde *à l'ancienne*
Old-Fashioned Mustard
250 ml

MAISON ORPHÉE

POUR LES SANDWICHS... ET PLUS
FOR SANDWICHES... AND MORE

BIOLOGIQUE ❧ ORGANIC

Moutarde jaune *au curcuma*
Yellow Mustard *with Turmeric*
250 ml

 Maison Orphée

Develop new packaging for Maison Orphée, a producer and importer of oils and condiments. The packaging strategy is based on the insight that consumers increasingly distinguish between everyday cooking products and gourmet serving products. The Gourmet line, which features high quality oils, is shown here.

Design Agency: *lg2boutique*. Production Date: *2010*. Creative Director: *Claude Auchu*. Designer: *Serge Côté*. Nationality: *Canada*.

Full Tank Baby Fuel

Full Tank Baby Fuel combines the benefits of home - prepared veggies with the convenience of portability. Baby Fuel packages the freshest organic ingredients in a travel-ready easy open squeeze pouches that fit in your pocket or purse and can be eaten without a spoon.

Design Agency: *Turnstyle.* Production Date: *2008.* Creative Director: *Steven Watson.* Designer: *Steven Watson.* Client: *Full Tank Foods.* Nationality: *USA.*

 Gracious Gourmet

Gracious Gourmet's extensive line of upscale condiments brings chef-quality flavours to the home cook. With minimalist typography, bright colours and plenty of white space, the distinctive packaging appeals to modern shoppers, while the super-sized botanical illustrations communicate the products' sense of homemade quality.

Design Agency: *Identity and Packaging for a Boutique Condiment Company.* Production Date: *2007.* Creative Director: *Matteo Bologna.* Art Director: *Andrea Brown.* Designer: *Andrea Brown.* Client: *The Gracious Gourmet.* Nationality: *USA.*

 **Organic Honey**

A product visualisation project showcasing a new and unique way to package honey. A clean, minimalistic logo and branding using an elegant and simple typefaces upon large white space or canvas gives the design a distinctive and sophisticated appeal. This is further emphasised by the gold embossed bee logo. The large white "canvas" is balanced with the golden warmth of the honey appearing through the glass at the base of the packaging.

Design Agency: *Circum Punkt Design*. Production Date: *2009*. Designer: *Marcel Buerkle*. Nationality: *South Africa*.

 Taj, Restartant, House Sauces

Taj Indian Gourmet is an upscale restaurant of India. The target audience is business
men, 30–55 middle to high class who are looking for sophistication and luxury. The
designer developed a hand made font to invoke this brand and added a lotus flower
to unify the visual concept of the identity. The colours applied were deep browns,
light blue and orange tones, predominant colours in India. The final result is a
sophisticated and interesting mark that describes the mood and the strong view of
this identity.

Design Agency: *Elo Designs*. Production Date: *2010*. Nationality: *USA*.

 PRIMVS Food

PRIMVS is a brand that has decided to up the ante in a number of consumer sectors. It has initially turned its attention to food, a sector that has, for too long, been looked upon as merely a necessity of life and requires limited in-depth packaging design. PRIMVS feels that design and form have been neglected in the way food packaging is presented and the PRIMVS Food brand aims to attract those who appreciate premium quality food and design. PRIMVS has merged quality food, with a minimalist stylised packaging that is both visually attractive and appealing. The launch of the PRIMVS Food brand will initially be exclusively in Japan, to be followed worldwide at a later date to be announced.

Design Agency: *Primvs Design.* Production Date: *2010.* Client: *Primvs Food.* Photography: *Primvs Design .* Nationality: *Italy.*

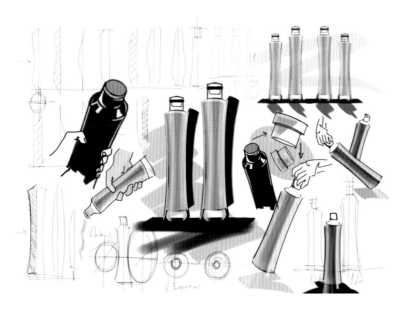

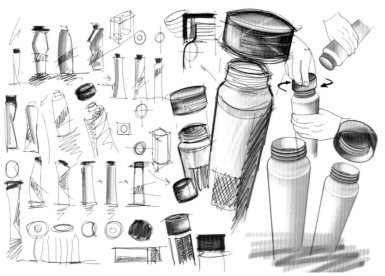

Bong

Distinctive design is helping the customer to make the "right choice". In a world when fine cooking at home has become everybody's hobby, where do you find the right bouillon? Bong's bouillon is out there, but what are they made of? Make the choice easy for the customer. And when the choice is made, the bouillon should be easy to use; important information uncomplicated to find. In this case, less really became more. The clarity has helped the customer to find the product they're looking for. And more often than before, they find Bong...

Design Agency: *Neumeister Strategic Design AB*. Production Date: *2010*. Creative Director: *Peter Neumeister*. Designer: *Peter Neumeister / Carl Larsson*. Client: *Campbell*. Nationality: *USA*.

Cooper's Kitchen

These jams and salads are part of a food line, Cooper's Kitchen, which originated in a country store in Barryville, New York founded by country singer Cooper Boone. Originally the products were sold in a simple mason jar with a generic crack and peel label. Biggs&Co. was approached to take the brand to the next level; allowing room for it to work like a mass market product line, but keeping the country store charm and appeal.

Classic country - inspired weathered fonts act as illustration, sprinkled with farm - inspired colours to identify the brand. You know you are buying a quality product that makes you feel like it was just made in a country kitchen.

Design Agency: *Biggs&Co.* Production Date: *2010.* Designer: *Alli Truch.* Client: *Cooper Boone.* Photography: *Gavin Jones.* Nationality: *USA.*

Gordon Ramsay Product Line

The assignment was to create an elegant product line for a famous chef. The designer chose Gordon Ramsay, a renowned England chef who has received 10 Michelin stars. For this, the designer utilised a clean and simple design that emphasised the typography as a differentiating element to accompany the photography. Instead of laying out the food as it would appear on a plate, it is placed in a more artistic manner as if it was a sculpture. The designer used photographs on the lateral panels of the boxes in order to create a more dynamic brand (example: escargots and marmalades). As you can see, it's a very clean, elegant and simple way to create a brand that is unified by a typographic style.

Design Agency: *Gworkshop.* Production Date: *2010.* Creative Director: *José Luis García Eguiguren.* Designer: *José Luis García Eguiguren.* Client: *Gordon Ramsay.* Nationality: *Ecuador.*

Smucker's Orchard's Finest

This new product offering of a premium fruit spread is targeted to compete with European and domestic premium spreads. The challenge was to convince gourmet conscious consumers that Smucker's high quality ingredients meet their need for great taste and a simple formula. The result is an ownable structural jar design and Orchard's Finest sub-brand name that carves out a distinctive space in the category.

Design Agency: *CIULLA ASSOC.* Production Date: *2009.* Creative Director: *Sam J. Ciulla.* Designer: *Julie Wineski / Luis Izaguirre.* Client: *J.M. Smucker Company.* Nationality: *USA.*

Traditional Spoon Sweet

An all time classic Greek delicacy-in essence boiled fruit in syrup-spoon(able) deserts are part of the country's DNA. Originally homemade, this unique product although simply made, is a culinary experience. Therefore, mouth-watering and straightforward was what the designers aimed for. A traditional for this type of sweets-glass jar was chosen, with a simple white label depicting the actual product ready for consumption. The idea was to merge traditional and modern, creating a strong appetite appeal. The designers wanted the consumer to desire the product, ideally immediately to unscrew the cap and eat it there and then before he has a chance to pay for it!

Design Agency: *Mousegraphics*. Production Date: *2009*. Creative Director: *Gregory Tsaknakis*. Illustrator: *Ioanna Papaioannou*. Client: *SARADIS*. Nationality: *Greece*.

Prima Luce Cerezas En Su Jugo

Selected cherries naturally preserved in their own juice prepared in traditional way: the design and specific wording on the label are orientated to impress the consumer with an innovative, natural and convenient product that has a long shelf life without the need for preservatives.

Design Agency: *Campoy Príncipi Domenech | CPD | Design & Calligraphy*. Production Date: *2010*. Creative Director: *Lucía Domenech*. Designer: *Lucía Domenech*. Client: *Frutta Roja*. Photography: *Gustavo Sabez*. Nationality: *Argentina*.

 Jardim D'oliveira

Jardim D'oliveira aims to be not only a simple and modern olive oil but also part of people lifestyle. It is a delicate DOP Trás-os-Montes 100% organic extra virgin olive oil with a pleasant taste of fresh olives and a beautiful golden colour. Jardim D'oliveira is a blend of stylish conceptual design and premium quality Portuguese olive oil. The design is minimalist and conceptual. The triangle shape is the biggest simplification of the olive tree shape. Jardim D'oliveira means Garden of Olive Trees in English. The pattern of triangles represents that garden.

Design Agency: *NTGJ.* Creative Director: *Guilherme Jardim.* Designer: *Guilherme Jardim / Pedro Andre / Vladimir Pospelov.* Client: *Jardim d'Oliveira.* Photography: *Vladimir Pospelov.* Nationality: *Portugal.*

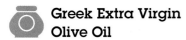

Greek Extra Virgin Olive Oil

Based on a brief that essentially could be distilled in two key ideas - Premium Quality & Visual Differentiation - this olive oil packaging targets an international high-end audience. In an otherwise crowded shelf space were all brands aim to convince the buyer by visually stating the obvious, this packaging is deliberately moving away from traditional symbols of olive oil quality or clichés of provenance. This packaging design targets the mind; aesthetics is the real reason to buy. Almost as an afterthought, a very realistic-looking drop of oil on the tin is what keeps it grounded into the food section of a super market; if ever there was a slogan attached to it, then this would read "simply, a good quality olive oil".

Design Agency: *Mousegraphics*. Production Date: *2009*. Creative Director: *Gregory Tsaknakis*. Designer: *Vassiliki Argyropoulou*. Client: *AGRO.VI.M.* Nationality: *Greece*.

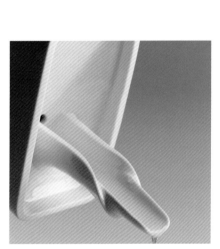

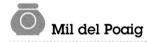 **Mil del Poaig**

Design of container for olive oil. Production from millenarian olive trees is calculated in around 3000 half - litre bottles per year. Distribution worldwide as a unique exclusive product. Design aims to communicate the history and tradition behind the product.

A very exclusive edition of a very special product. All aspects of its packaging communicate the product high quality standards and attributes: natural character, extra virgin quality, purity and beauty of the fluid. The pouring system allows the fluid show off with sensuality, colour, texture and rhythm.

500 millilitre olive oil bottle in white porcelain inside a cardboard box.

Design Agency: *El Poaig*. Production Date: *2008*. Nationality: *Spain*.

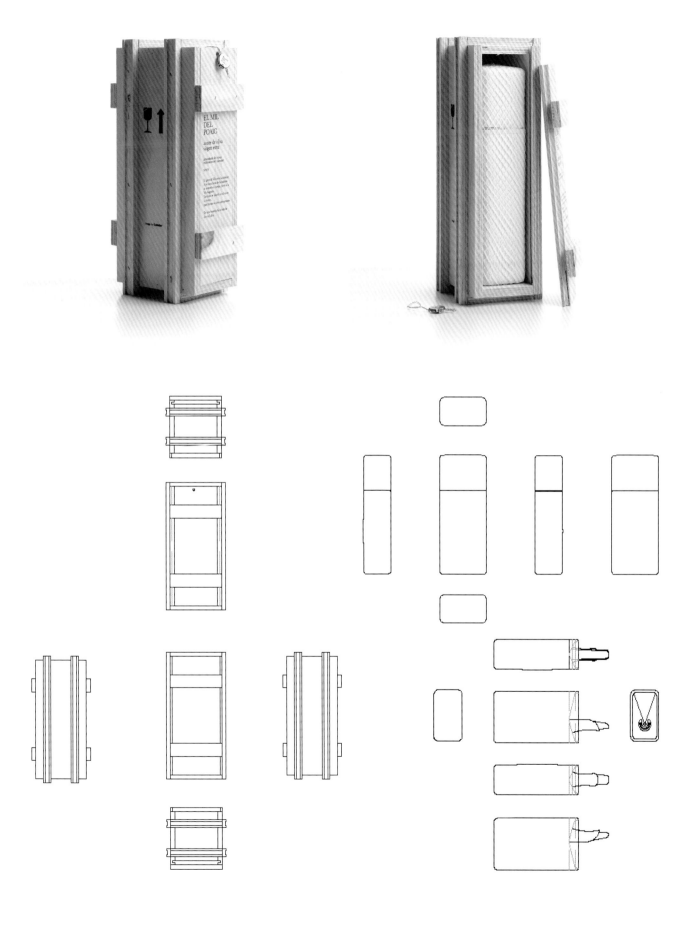

 Verd del Poaig

Design of container for olive oil. Production from millenarian olive trees is calculated in around 3000 half - litre bottles per year. Distribution worldwide as a unique exclusive product. Design aims to communicate the history and tradition behind the product.

A very exclusive edition of a very special product. All aspects of its packaging communicate the product high quality standards and atributes: natural character, extra virgin quality, purity and beauty of the fluid. The pouring system allows the fluid show off with sensuality, colour, texture and rythm.

250 millilitre olive oil bottle in white porcelain inside a cardboard box.

Design Agency: *El Poaig*. Production Date: *2010*. Nationality: *Spain*.

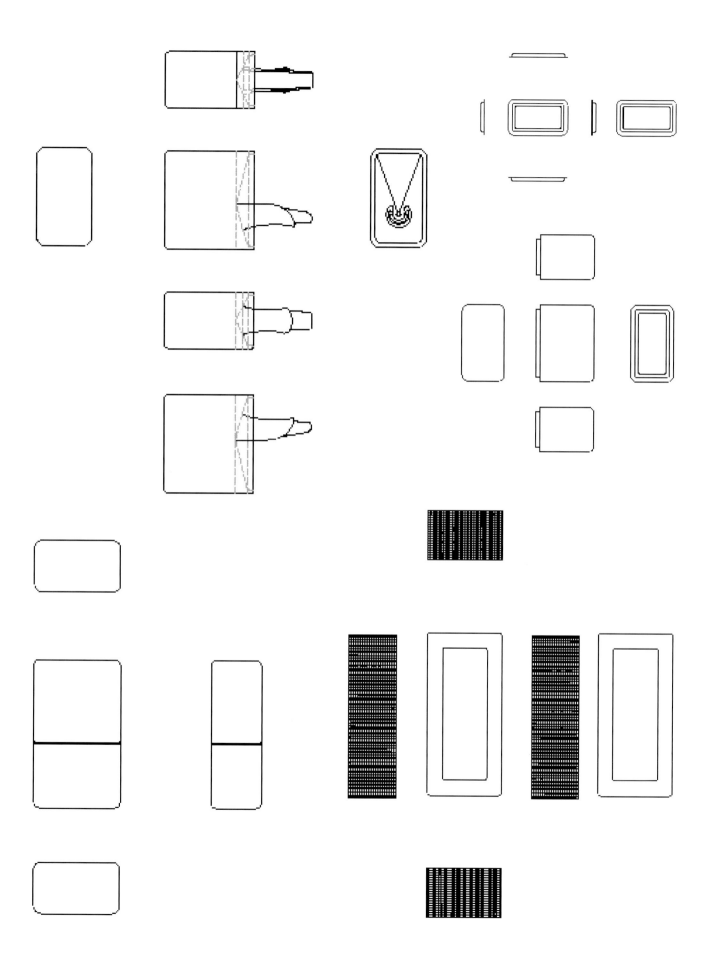

 Sheffield Honey Company

Sheffield Honey Company "is an artisan producer of premium quality local English honey and beeswax products" and sells Blossom, Soft Set and Heather honey. DED pay a subtle homage to Sheffield's (England) industrial past with a simple, utilitarian approach to its very own honey brand. Sheffield Honey Company brand's mark straddles between a nut (as in "and bolt") and a honeycomb and is purposely understated.

Design Agency: *DED Associates*. Production Date: *2010–2011*. Designer: *Nik Daughtry / Jon Daughtry / Rob Barber*. Client: *Sheffield Honey Company*. Photography: *Nik Daughtry*. Nationality: *UK*.

 Hashi

There is a huge selection of "Hashi" hot sauces: a very hot "Halapenio", extremely hot "Habanero", unbearable hot sauce "Cayenne pepper", as well as wasabi and mustard. That special look "#@$#!" was created just as soon as the designers tried this hot sauce at the studio. Hattomonkey informal packaging design is hot and excited. This is not just a simple sauce on a store shelf; it shouts the same language you do "#@$#!".

Designer: *Hattomonkey / Alexey Kurchin*. Client: *Interra LTD*. Nationality: *Russia*.

 Passanha Olive Oil

Michael Young was commissioned by Base Design and Passanha Oil to design this new glass bottle. The Passanha brand dates to 1749 and this bottle marks the re-launch of this historical olive oil company. Passanha brothers Luis and Joao Felipe decided to revive the family tradition, in updated packaging that was contemporary yet linked to the family heritage. The brothers invested in a new olive press, and are today the only olive oil company in Portugal controlling the entire chain of production-from tree to bottle.

By incorporating the new logo that Base Design has created, this olive oil bottle is divided into upper and lower parts by a horizontal ridge with the "drop" just below, representing the olive press and at the same time emphasising the oil and its colour.

Design Agency: *Michael Young Ltd.* Production Date: *2010.* Designer: *Michael Young.* Client: *Herdeiros Passanha.* Nationality: *Hong Kong (China).*

QSV Colheita Premium and Dom Diogo

The designers built the packaging respecting the brand they created around a few key elements: a drop, round logo, a contemporary stencil typeface, a relevant colour code, and imagery of the family estate. The bottle, designed by Michael Young, is conceived as an olive press, with an upper and lower part.

Design Agency: *Basedesign*. Production Date: *2010*. Client: *Passanha Herdeiros Olive Oil*. Photography: *Lydie Nesvadba / Julien Claessens*. Nationality: *Hong Kong (China)*.

 GLORIOUS! Soup

The design agency, ilovedust worked on the GLORIOUS! Soup rebrand with TSC Foods and Lambie-Naim recently and were very proud of the results! An iconic illustration style was created for each letter of the alphabet, representing the authentic global influences and flavours of each product. For example, within the soup range, T is for "Toulouse Sausage and Bean" and M stands for "Malaysian Chicken". Mark Graham, Creative Director at ilovedust: "We had a lot of fun with the new GLORIOUS! branding with so many interesting ingredients to work with and global locations to take inspiration from, we were spoilt for choice on what we could do graphically."

Design Agency: *ilovedust*. Production Date: *2010*. Nationality: *UK*.

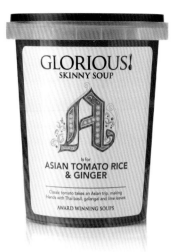

GLORIOUS!
SKINNY SOUP

Is for
ASIAN TOMATO RICE
& GINGER

Classic tomato takes an Asian trip, making
friends with Thai basil, galangal and lime leaves

AWARD WINNING SOUPS

GLORIOUS!
SKINNY SOUP

Is for
FRAGRANT THAI CARROT
& LEMONGRASS

Fresh and fabulous; a light and breezy fusion
of coconut, turmeric and lime leaves

AWARD WINNING SOUPS

GLORIOUS!
SKINNY SOUP

Is for
GOAN SPICED
TOMATO & LENTIL

Warm and laid-back, with cumin, coriander and
turmeric putting a little Indian pep in its step

AWARD WINNING SOUPS

GLORIOUS!
SKINNY SOUP

Is for
NEW ENGLAND
BUTTERNUT SQUASH

An East Coast secret; unexpectedly light and smooth,
with warm cumin, peppy paprika and a flash of mango

AWARD WINNING SOUPS

GLORIOUS!
SOUP

Is for
MALAYSIAN
CHICKEN

An exotic adventure, where coconut
is seduced by chilli and lemongrass

AWARD WINNING SOUPS

GLORIOUS!
SOUP

Is for
SUNNY THAI
CHICKEN

Taste the sunshine in this fusion of sweet potato,
spinach and aromatic thai spices

AWARD WINNING SOUPS

GLORIOUS!
PASTA SAUCE

NEW YORK
ALFREDO SAUCE

An Italian-American classic featuring
parmigiano reggiano, co-starring
peppers and mushrooms

 Fruta del Diablo Salsa Packaging

There are a wide variety of salsas in the marketplace, with offerings from small startups and international corporations alike vying for consumer dollars. Moxie Sozo wanted to create salsa packaging for Fruta del Diablo that would distinguish it from everything else on the shelf and establish credibility for an unknown brand. By using hand-drawn illustrations inspired by the woodcuts of Mexican artist Jose Guadalupe Posada, the designers were able to lend authenticity to the salsa while reinforcing the product's heritage in traditional Mexican cuisine.

Design Agency: *Moxie Sozo*. Production Date: *2008*. Creative Director: *Leif Steiner*. Designer: *Nate Dyer*. Client: *Fruta del Diablo*. Nationality: *USA*.

 **Kikkoman**

Shown are conceptual bottles for a high-end line of infused soy sauces.

Designer: *Jon Patterson.* Photography: *Jon Patterson.*
Nationality: *USA.*

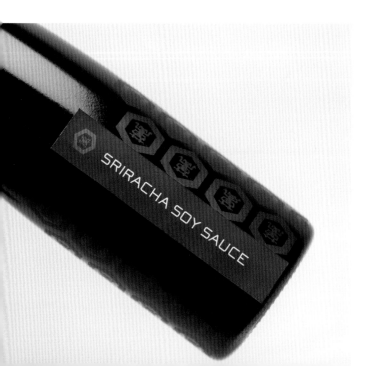

Grenny's Secret

Peter Gregson Studio completely redesigned the Granny's Secret line of traditionally made products from the Serbian food company "Foodland". That included both the label and the glass containers. Designer's goal was to create a design that would remind people of home-made food products as made by their grandmas. Glass jars and bottles as well as the label communicate the natural, human and emotional platform of the brand.

Production Date: *2011*. Art Director: *Jovan Trkulja / Marijana Zaric*. Designer: *Jovan Trkulja / Marijana Zaric*. Client: *Foodland*. Nationality: *Serbia*.

Evolve Cold Pressed Oils

SabotagePKG have designed the brand & structural identity for a new range of premium, organic, cold pressed oils by Evolve. The brief was to create an ecological-premium brand identity which embodies this ethos. Sabotage developed a chic 330 millilitre/11.16 fluid ounce carafe style glass bottle complete with integral lid and pour spout lid. The bottle has been designed with reuse in mind and in this way reducing ecological impact. Oil refills come in a seal fresh pouch. The base oil range includes Hemp Seed, Walnut, Apricot Kernel & Pumpkin Seed each individually identified by a colour code system.

Design Agency: *SabotagePKG.* Production Date: *2011.* Designer: *SabotagePKG.* Client: *Evolve Brands.* Photography: *Studio 21 London.* Nationality: *England.*

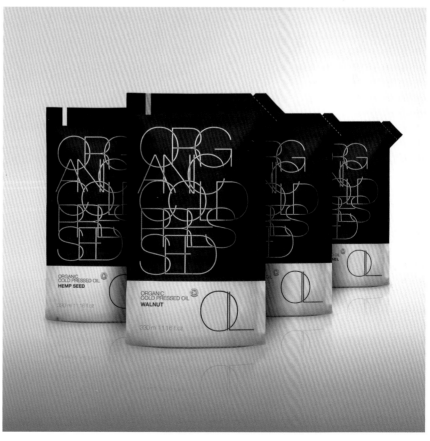

 **Guzman Y Gomez Mexican Sauce
Packaging**

A range of own brand Mexican sauces using existing brand guidelines and current
employees to highlight authenticity and personality.

The solution was to capture store employees tasting the various sauces and
photograph their reactions. The facial expressions reflect the strength and potency
of the sauce while also introducing a member of the staff, and gives great cut-
through on shelf. Captions printed on the bottle sides link the staff to the sauce
through their own personal history with the Mexican product. The black and white
imagery ties in with the store look and feel whilst creating a better platform for using
nonprofessional models.

Design Agency: *The Creative Method*. Production Date: *2008*. Creative Director:
Tony Ibbotson. Art Director: *Tony Ibbotson / Andi Yanto*. Designer: *Tony Ibbotson
/ Andi Yanto*. Client: *Guzman Y Gomez*. Photography: *Andrew Gash*. Nationality:
Australia.

Fuego Hot Sauce

Fuego Hot Sauce was designed to educate people about the Scoville Scale and inform them about the types, uses, and ways to use hot sauce in an engaging and exciting experience. The designer wanted to evoke the authentic feel of the sauces and showcase their natural colours and flavours. By giving the product a sturdy bottle and hearty labeling system, people can feel confident using the product and know exactly what heat level they use according to the scaling system. Each blend is made of completely different peppers and ingredients so that they each pair well with a different kind of food. The Fuego Heat Guide and Recipe book further explains the background of each pepper and suggests recipes that correspond with each unique flavour.

Production Date: *2010*. Designer: *Stephanie Hughes*.
Client: *University of Washington*. Nationality: *USA*.

 Clearspring Oils

Establish Clearspring as the premium organic brand in the England 20 to 45-year-old consumers who want the food they eat to be good and taste good. Simple eye-catching premium packaging design for a range of high-end organic oils. A subtle integration of die-cut label and structure helps create standout, showing clear differentiation in a traditionally "folksy" market.

Design Agency: *Mayday (London)*. Production Date: *2009*. Creative Director: *Roger Akroyd*. Designer: *Barry Gillibrand*. Client: *Clearspring Organic*. Nationality: *UK*.

Womersley Herb Vinegars

The brief was to rebrand the range of fruit and herb vinegars and jellies, reinforcing the brands heritage and gourmet credentials and also making it a desirable "foodie" gift. At the centre of the redesign is a stylised "W". It acts as a pictorial "trellis" against which the fruit and herb imagery grows. Swedish artist Petra Börner was commisioned to create the botanical illustrations which alongside the contemporary colour palette and elegant typography convey a sense of Womersley's position in the market as a modern food producer with a traditional heritage.

Design Agency: *Mayday (London).* Production Date: *2010.* Creative Director: *Roger Akroyd.* Designer: *Barry Gillibrand.* Illustrator: *Petra Borner.* Client: *Womersley Fine Foods.* Nationality: *England.*

le verger
en poésie

fabrication
artisanale
confiture
350 gr

artiste culinaire & four

 Atelier Bidule

Graphic design and production for the brand culinary Amb (logotype, business
card, packaging, web site). They have worked around the greedy letter.

Design Agency: *Atelier Bidule*. Production Date: *2010*. Creative Director: *Cécile
Stollini–Gay / Sidney Gay*. Art Director: *Cécile Stollini–Gay / Sidney Gay*. Designer:
Damien Gibot. Client: *AMB*. Photography: *Atelier Bidule*. Nationality: *France*.

fabriqué en France.
ingrédients : fruits 60 %, sucre 40 %,
gélifiant : pectine, acidifiant : jus de citron.
à consommer de préférence avant : voir capsule.
tenir au frais après ouverture.
www.vergerenpoesie.fr

AMB

aveur

Auberginenkaviar
Caviar d'aubergine

Andreas Caminada

Andreas Caminada is an exceptionally gifted chef who was awarded 19 Gault Millau Points and was chosen two times as chef of the year in Switzerland in 2008 and 2010 by the Gault Millau Guide. The modular - based icons and the texts on the backside invite you to a special world of delicious food in a special atmosphere. Triangle, square and line, also sometimes a small circle: that is the vocabulary for the modular sketching. Next to the ingredients and the serving suggestions, wild little stories can be read on the back of the packaging. They are confusing, they make you smile and some are a bit eerie. No surprise if you know that Andreas Caminada is cooking in a castle.

Design Agency: *STUDIO Remo Caminada*. Production Date: *2009*. Designer: *Donat Caduff / Remo Caminada / Michael Häne*. Client: *Andreas Caminada, Switzerland*. Photography: *Thomas de Monaco*. Nationality: *Switzerland*.

Kalb-Reduktion
Réduction de veau

Gemüseessenz
Essence de légumes

Ingwer mit Gewürzen
Gingembre aux épices

Mandeltuille
Tuile d'amande

Tomatenmojo
Mojo de tomates

Schwarze Nüsse
Noix noires de Pécan

Peperoniconfit
Piment confit

Safranessenz
Essence au safran

Schokococo-Tuille

Two souls live in one of the best-beloved and well-known products worldwide: Nutella. A legendary, playful, imaginative soul lives with a nutritious one. Nutella's cult is celebrated thanks to its limited editions, too, which mark year-round pivotal moments. ARC'S designed the packaging for Nutella Carnival + Easter 2008 and Carnival 2009 editions for the Italian market, setting a modern, fresh, and elegant style.

Design Agency: *ARC'S.* Production Date: *2008–2009.*
Creative Directors: *Lino Bergesio / Stefano Zimbaro.*
Designer: *Roberto Blefari / Giulia Gioanola / Angelo Iannuzzi.* Client: *Ferrero Italia.* Nationality: *Italy.*

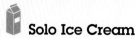

Solo Ice Cream

Solo is a small ice cream lab in Northern Israel, where
fine ice cream is made from local ingredients and by
traditional Italian methods. The branding is designed
to convey simplicity on one hand and quality on the
other hand; from raw material to the final product.

Design Agency: *Kroll.* Production Date: *2010.* Creative
Director: *Dov Kroll.* Designer: *Dov Kroll.* Client: *Solo
Ice Cream.* Photography: *Yasmin & Arye–Studio Ya.*
Nationality: *Israel.*

Good Milk

Milk is a universal and indispensable product. Going along with the modern
tendency to popularise healthy lifestyles and recognising the importance of
environmental protection, the designers suggest that this product, serving all
peoples well since times immemorial, should be super-popularly served in
aluminium cans.

Their advantages include light weight and strength, aesthetical appearance and
compactness. Aluminium cans fully preserve the natural taste and quality of the
product and are easily opened. Because of the new design of the packaging, milk
may not be just served at home but also taken along anywhere.

Within the same concept, the designers also suggest a possible extension of the
technology of the production of the Tetra Pak packaging. The idea is using Congreve
stamping in the production of regular milk cartons.

The design of the whole line is built on the contrast between the colour of the logo
with the predominant white, which, as we see it, goes just fine with the product. The
soft pastel colours are either lighter or darker depending on fat content and may
differ according to varying tastes. The appearance of the packaging will make this
traditional product go well with the modern times and make a room for it among
the popular beverages of the latest generations.

Because milk is so good for everyone and because of the radically new packaging,
Goodmilk may now be called a super-drink.

Design Agency: *StudioIN*. Production Date: *2010*. Art Director: *Arthur Schreiber*.
Designer: *Maria Ponomareva*. Nationality: *Russia*.

 BioQ

The Norwegian dairy brand "Q" launched a new yoghurt drink called BioQ. The packaging of the drink shall communicate the values of the product, which are: natural, healthy, Norwegian, delicious yoghurt drink. For the packaging the designers combined the ancient Norwegian painting tradition "rosemaling" with modern elements and created a peculiar illustration which curls around the package. With the hand - drawn parts of the illustration and the brown paper background they established a home-made feeling that is far away from mass production. The unbleached paper refers to natural ingredients, and combined with fresh colours and fruits the designers achieved a balanced expression that visualises the values of the company. The plastic bows on top of the packaging are a new communication possibility on a packaging. They achieved a high clarity of colours on the bows as well as on the packaging which draws attention in the supermarket shelves. The product is produced in three different flavours: blueberry-aloe vera, blueberry raspberry, raspberry-cranberry.

Design Agency: *Bleed*. Production Date: *2008*. Creative Director: *Dag Solhaug*. Designer: *Astrid Feldner*. Client: *Q Meieriene*. Photography: *Divers*. Nationality: *Norway*.

Wegmans Yogurt Container

The main challenge with the current yogurt packaging was peeling the foil top off. The current tab is difficult to grip and pull especially for people who have less dexterity. By enlarging the tab, not only does it give a better grip, but it also provides a broad flat surface for brand identity. This solution is powerful, yet simple and intuitive to help the target audience peel the foil and access the contents of the package. The larger tab also has a strong visual impact in the shelves. Ultimately, it will benefit both companies and the consumers.

Design Agency: *Hyung Jin Choi*. Production Date: *2010*. Creative Director: *Hyung Jin Choi*. Designer: *Hyung Jin (Gina) Choi*. Nationality: *South Korea*.

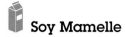 **Soy Mamelle**

Project participants (project organiser was PDA) were offered to design a creative brand conception for innovative product-soy milk, possessing unique functional advantages. The KIAN brand agency took on the process of naming, formulating a creative brand conception, and creating the package shape. Soy milk "Soy mamelle" is a 100% vegetative product. It is a source of high grade fibre and calcium, containing no cholesterol and a proven ability to actually lower cholesterol levels in the human body.

The developed conception of the package shape resembled an udder, which presents the first half of the message in that soy milk is identical to that of a cow. The second part of the message is delivered via the colour score and décor of the packaging, which concentrates on the phytogenesis of the product, creating an image of nature and health. The package can be made of a PET or a glass. It has convenient lid and leans on a three legs. This finding has tremendous potential for improvement of brand identity in POS materials and nonstandard equipment trading.

Design Agency: *KIAN Brand Agency*. Production Date: *2009*. Creative Director: *Mary Sypko*. Designer: *Evgeny Morgalev*. Client: *Pan European Brand Design Association (PDA)*. Nationality: *Russia*.

This is a non-commercial project oriented towards the creation of a decent mass-consumer-oriented product. The reserved classical design mostly emphasises the large images of tasty berries flooded with air-light yogurt. The product pleases various tastes by its colour variety and the carefully selected pleasant to the eye juicy hues.

Design Agency: *StudioIN*. Production Date: *2010*. Art Director: *Arthur Schreiber*. Designer: *Maria Ponomareva*. Nationality: *Russia*.

Arla Milk Bottle

A true challenge. How do the designers get people on the run to buy milk? Arla, the largest producer of dairy products in Scandinavia, wanted milk to have a life outside the traditional stores. Milk, next to coke, juice or whatever, in the rapidly growing fast food market.

The designers developed a brand new bottle and packaging structure. Obviously a flirt with the traditional milkman and his bottle, but with an unquestionably modern touch. Innocent white being the main colour of attraction, making the individual green, blue etc, important tools of communication.

The launch made a strong impression in the fast-food segment, making milk a healthier alternative to other beverages.

Design Agency: *Neumeister Strategic Design AB.*
Production Date: *1998.* Designer: *Peter Neumeister.*
Client: *Arla.* Nationality: *Sweden.*

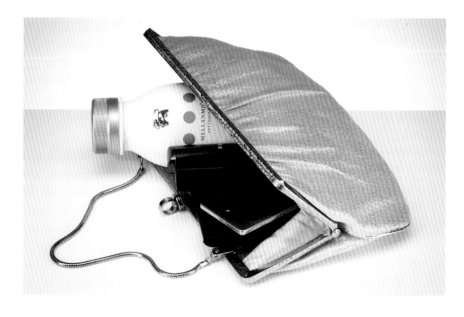

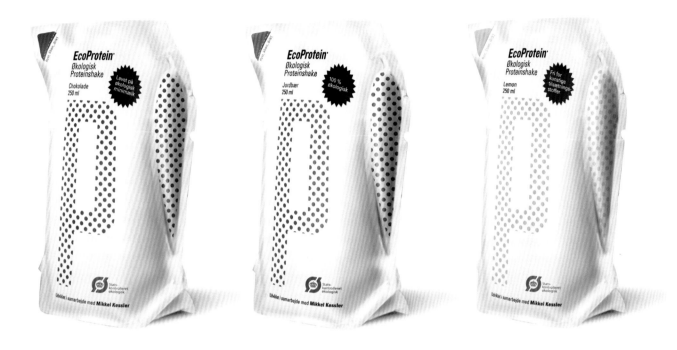

EcoProtein

P is for protein and in Denmark is for Organic (kologisk). EcoProtein is Denmark's first organic whey protein powder, developed in corporation with Super middleweight World Champion Mikkel Kessler. The product is clean and without any artificial flavours, colouring or sugars. This was the inspiration for a clean design with no unnecessary elements. The halftone pattern a graphic interpretation of the powder itself, simply changing colour with the flavour/content. The logotype custom made to have the right look and feel with catchy detailing and character.

Production Date: *2010–2011*. Designer: *Mads Jakob Poulsen*. Client: *EcoProtein / Copenhagen Denmark*. Nationality: *Denmark*.

Mew: Cereal Soy Milk

A new cereal soy milk product to market to young urban people who enjoy a fun lifestyle. The packaging shows a fun activity for each flavour.

Design Agency: *Default Bangkok*. Production Date: *2010*. Designer: *Rapeeparn Kitnichee*. Nationality: *USA*.

 **Cowmilk**

People used to mention embroidery on material not on paper. That's why such a cross stitch package attracts attention. As you may see the peculiarities of package construction let to create cow ears. That makes a new package become notable among others. The designers made simple and highlighted package concept, which gratefully introduces your product on a shelf.

Designer: *Hattomonkey / Alexey Kurchin*. Client: *Milk Collection*. Nationality: *Russia*.

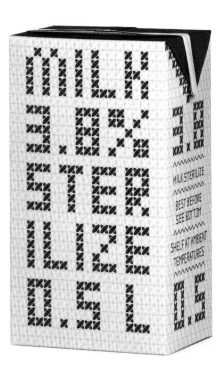

Crestmilk

Hattomonkey design studio has created a brand new dairy beverage product package concept. So the task which has been set before designers is to invent a package, which is to underline naturality, thereby to get closer to the consumer of diary products. The idea was born unexpectedly: to stylise package by a cross stitch.

Designer: *Hattomonkey / Alexey Kurchin.* Client: *Milk Collection.* Nationality: *Russia.*

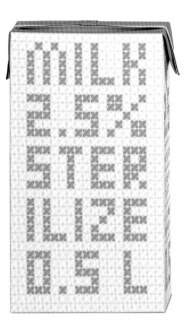

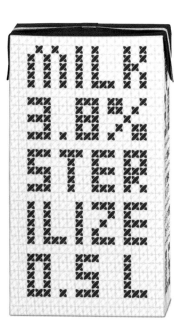

On the package:

Open here

Milk cocktail by Joe

Strawberry

Wheat Flour, Vegetable Oil(Palm Oil, Rapeseed, Soy and Corn Oil), Sugar, Lactose, Whole Milk Powder, Shortening, Butter, Salt, Dried Strawberry, Skim Milk Powder, Dextrin, Artificial Flavor(Strawberry and Milk), Red Beet Color, Soy Lecithin, Trisodium, Phosphate, Sodium Bicarbonate, Contains Milk, Wheat, and Soy

300 ml

 Milk Cocktail by Joe / Batmilk

Hattomonkey has created a packaging design of milk cocktail "by Joe". It looks like well-known hero. It is easy to create Batman's ears. Hattomonkey designers have created a brand new package form. It looks familiar and well-known since childhood.

Designer: *Hattomonkey / Alexey Kurchin.* Client: *Milk Collection.* Nationality: *Russia.*

 Ella Milk Products

The designers have a meaning that market is overloaded with wrong packaging design especially for low fat dairy products, and that is why they wanted to design something completely different.

They have chosen derivative style with fine, serif typography and simple colours. Since the product is mostly consumed by women, the design has elements that remind of women magazines and fashion iconography. With this new and progressive packaging the designers want to inflect the consumer's expectations and make them more aware of the nature of this product.

Production Date: *2009*. Art Director: *Jovan Trkulja*. Designer: *Marijana Zaric*. Client: *Mlekara Subotica*. Nationality: *Serbia*.

Bara Goat Dairy

Bara is a small family dairy in Northern Israel. The flying goat portrays the essence of this product. As the central image of this design, it emphasises the attention invested into the well-being of the farm animals, creating a rich, sustainable product.

Design Agency: *Kroll*. Production Date: *2011*. Creative Director: *Dov Kroll*. Designer: *Dov Kroll*. Client: *Bara Dairy*. Photography: *Yasmin & Arye-Studio Ya*. Nationality: *Israel*.

 Milk Packaging

....

Experiment in cardboard packaging as well as in communication. It represents
the content of the product in the simplest way, both through word and image. The
packaging is the same dimension as a two litre milk carton.
Made in collaboration with Gabriel Lefebvre.

Design Agency: *Julien de Repentigny / Visual Advice*. Production Date: 2008.
Creative Director: *Julien de Repentigny*. Designer: *Julien de Repentigny*.
Photography: *Julien de Repentigny*. Nationality: *Canada*.

....

 Oatrageous

The object of this project was to create a new image for oatmeal in order to better position it in a market for women ages (25-35). Building on the "healthy and delicious" appeal of oatmeal, the designer utilised images to visually depict the ingredients: milk, fruit and oatmeal. The slight curve in the cup is not only more ergonomic but it also insinuates a thinning waistline. The tin foil covering the top of the cup will differentiate each flavour as each fruit is represented by a different colour.

Design Agency: *Gworkshop*. Production Date: 2010. Creative Director: *José Luis García Eguiguren*. Designer: *José Luis García Eguiguren*. Client: *Quaker Oats*. Photography: *Stock images*. Nationality: *Ecuador*.

Our Farm Diary

The small factory makes dairy products of the highest quality - without additives or preservatives, from non-polluting milk, very small parties and under the order. Labels and bottle shape reminiscent of home milk from grandma.

Design Agency: *Nadie Parshina Studio*. Production Date: 2009. Creative Director: *Nadie Parshina*. Designer: *Nadie Parshina*. Client: *KM–Elit*. Nationality: *Russia*.

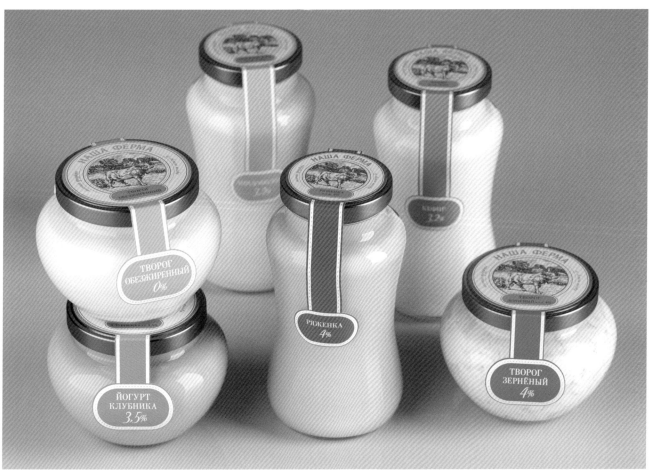

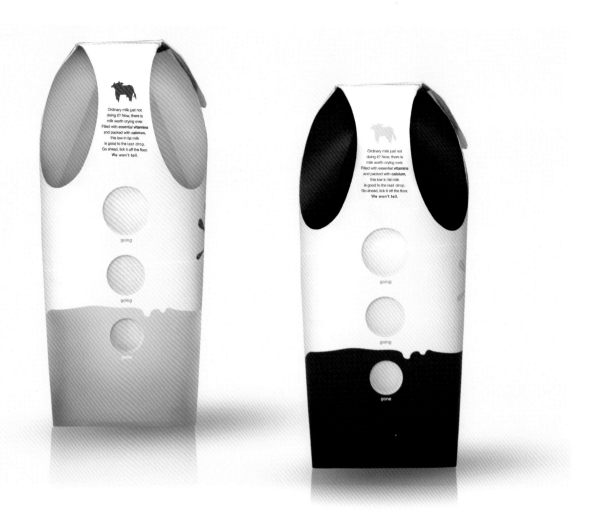

 Spilt Milk

"Ordinary milk just not doing it? Now, there is milk worth crying over. Filled with essential vitamins and packed with calcium, this low - in - fat milk is good to the last drop. Go ahead, lick it off the floor, we won't tell."

Packaging for Spilt Milk was constructed with the standard milk carton packaging in mind. To achieve a sleek, beautiful look, a bright and noticeable concept was desired. An innovative die-line was created to enhance the silhouette of the rectangular box. The curve-linear quality of the carton creates sex-appeal and modernity to the everyday dairy product. The circular elements create dimension, highlights and shadows that intrigue the eye to the product.

Three circular windows labelled "going, going, gone" allow you to see how much milk remains inside the container.

The carton is made from a thick cardboard paper coated with wax. The wax coating helps keep the product fresh as well as prevents the cardboard from absorbing liquid. The materials used were an "eco-conscious" choice as it makes container more easily disposable compared to a plastic. There is a small plastic snap at the spout-flap that allows you to open and reseal the container with ease. When pouring, the milk travels through the container where the spout opens and widens with the pressure of the flowing liquid.

Design Agency: *Wilfong Design.* Production Date: *2010.* Creative Director: *Jasmine Wilfong.* Designer: *Jasmine Wilfong.* Client: *FIDM.* Photography: *Jolisa Wilfong.* Nationality: *USA.*

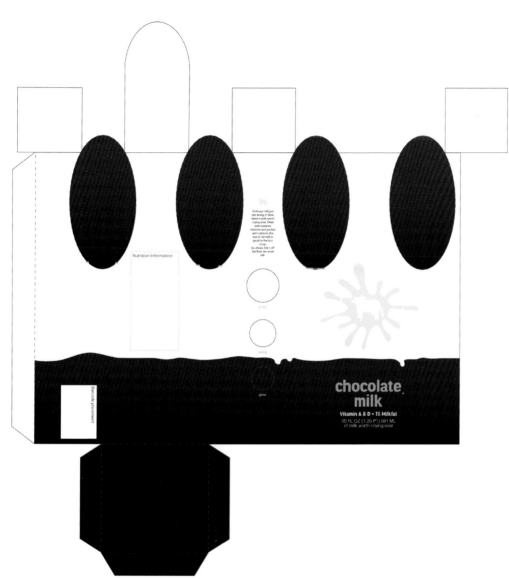

Nutrition Information

Ordinary milk just not doing it? Now, there is milk worth crying over. Filled with essential vitamins and packed with calcium, this low-in-fat milk is good to the last drop. Go ahead, lick it off the floor, we won't tell.

Barcode placement

g1 thu

going

gone

chocolate milk

Vitamin A & D • 1% Milkfat
20 FL OZ (1.25 PT) 591 ML
of milk worth crying over

$pilt

vanilla milk

Vitamin A & D • 1% Milkfat
20 FL OZ (1.25 PT) 591 mL
of milk worth crying over

Fulga

The client asked initially for a "no cow" design for his new milk brand. He was ultimately conquered by the designers' proposal of Fulga - the cheeky, one-of-a-kind, and now legendary little cow. Irreverently showing her back on the (back of the) package, Fulga became shortly a well - loved rebel, and brought an astounding success to its owner.

Design Agency: *Brandient.* Production Date: 2005. Creative Director: *Cristian 'Kit' Paul.* Designer: *Cristian 'Kit' Paul / Bogdan Dumitrache.* Illustration: *Iuliana Valsan.* Client: *Albalact SA.* Nationality: *Romania.*

Wine Awakenings

Mookai recently rebranded Wine Awakenings, a unique company specialising in wine education and leisure learning. Popular with sommeliers, culinary experts and wine lovers, the company offers a series of wine aroma kits designed to enhance one's ability to identify the aromas found in wine.

Mookai created the new identity to reflect the sensory experience of wine tasting and scenting. The illustrative style became a main branding element and was incorporated across the other materials. The Wine Aroma Kits were repackaged with matte black paper and the logos were foil stamped in colours representing the different wine varieties. Inside the kit are the aroma vials, an informative brochure and a set of illustrated sent cards which further assist in enhancing the wine tasting experience.

Design Agency: *Mookai Communications.* Production Date: *2010.* Creative Director: *Lori von Sychowski.* Art Director: *Lori von Sychowski.* Designer: *Tanya Duffy.* Client: *Wine Awakenings.* Photography: *Carlo Hindian.* Nationality: *Canada.*

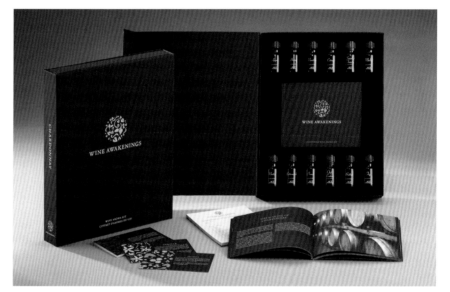

JAQK Cellars

JAQK Cellars is a new wine brand that wraps one thing people love - wine - inside another, gaming. This lifestyle approach to branding wine is virtually unheard of in the industry, creating a huge opportunity to stand out in a hopelessly crowded category. Hatch named the company, as well as each wine, and positioned it under the tag line, "Play a Little." The designers did all design work and sourced all materials, going as far as finding a specialty glass boutique in Milan to create the customised bottle for the flagship Cabernet. They also created a strongly branded e-commerce website that leverages the design aesthetics to make this new lifestyle wine brand accessible, desirable and attainable. To round out the experience, the designers designed gift boxes, apparel and a limited edition deck of JAQK playing cards.

Design Agency: *Hatch Design.* Production Date: *2007.* Creative Director: *Katie Jain/ Joel Templin.* Designer: *Joel Templin / Katie Jain / Eszter T. Clark / Ryan Meis.* Client: *JAQK Cellars.* Nationality: *USA.*

 ## Cabo Unotequila Anego Reserva

Meat and Potatoes sourced all elements of the packaging to be made in Mexico. "Our goal was to create a luxury yet authentic feel to the packaging." Housed in a handmade leather and wood box, the cork-sealed bottle comes with a crystal stopper. Each bottle of this limited edition of 21,000 bottles is numbered the earmark its allocated status as "authentic, elegant Mexican". This bottle retails for 225.00 US dollar.

Design Agency: *Meat and Potatoes, Inc.* Creative Director: *Todd Gallopo / TJ River.* Art Director: *TJ River / Todd Gallopo.* Designer: *TJ River / Todd Gallopo / Johnny Hsu.* Client: *Cabo Wabo Tequila.* Photography: *Meat and Potatoes, Inc.* Nationality: *USA.*

Grappa Norton. Bodega Norton

Label design is not simply dressing the bottle; it implies the understanding of the product in order to design a label that will satisfy the consumers, and in this case the designers need to communicate elegance and innovation at the same time.
The label is all printed on the bottle, so the designers could play with the effect that produces the image printed on the glass.

Design Agency: *Estudio Iuvaro*. Production Date: *2007*. Designer: *Cecilia Iuvaro*.
Client: *Bodega Norton*. Photography: *Federico Garcia*. Nationality: *Argentina*.

 Oscar's

Oscar's Gin emerged as a response to a brief for a premium product with intriguing packaging and an engaging background story. Oscar Wilde is used as the hypothetical company's identity, as he instantly communicates elegance and good taste. This premium London Dry Gin has been created in honour of Oscar, one who appreciated the finer things in life (and was a renowned drinker of gin). The packaging concept is featured around a quote by Wilde – "We are all in the gutter but some of us are looking at the stars." This is illustrated visually through layers and the unique glass which in a certain light has the distinct appearance of a starry night sky.

Production Date: *2010.* Designer: *Hilary Sloane.* Client: *RMIT.* Nationality: *Australia.*

Breuckelen Gin

Breuckelen Distilling Company asked the designers to work with them on the branding of their new bottles and packaging. Breuckelen Distilling is an artisan distillery located in Brooklyn, New York. They handcraft delicious gin from organic New York grains, entirely within their Brooklyn location. Breuckelen is a tiny fraction of the size of typical distilleries but their production methods create products of the highest quality. Breuckelen's founder, Brad Estabrooke, is an ordinary guy with an extraordinary love of distinctive wines and spirits. He began studying the art of distilling almost two years ago now, and his passion for it has grown exponentially since his studies began.

Design Agency: *ilovedust.* Production Date: *2010.* Client: *Breuckelen Distilling Company.* Nationality: *UK.*

 Alternative

To name and create a premium organic package for a limited edition of top end
organic Marlborough Sauvignon Blanc Wine. It needed to look and feel natural but
original and act as a talking point for consumers.

Alternative was chosen as it reflects a new way of looking at organic packaging. The
concept simply shows a vine from the leaves, to the bark to the wine. Every aspect of
the packaging was organic, including the lazer - cut balsa wood, the string and wax
that is used to afix the label to the bottle, the outer paper wrapping and even the
inks used to print the image.

Creative Director: *Tony Ibbotson*. Designer: *Tony Ibbotson / Tim Heyer*. Client: *The
Creative Method*. Nationality: *Australia*.

Build Your Own

The aim was to create a unique gift to give the clients at Christmas and to act as a new business introduction. It needed to remind them of who the designers are and the long hours that they put into the work. It needed to feature all of the staff, reflect the creativity and sense of humour. The print run was 5,000 labels.

The designers obtained high quality cleanskin wines and created the own labels. Each label was based on one staff member. It included a number of facial features and the client is encouraged to BYO - Build Their Own. The wine and the label is the perfect substitute for when the real thing cannot be there.

Creative Director: *Tony Ibbotson*. Designer: *Andi Yanto*. Client: *The Creative Method*. Nationality: *Australia*.

Layers–Alcohol Designed for Women

Alcohol designed for women. Based on the phrase: "in vino veritas" (in wine there is the truth). Much like in this project the phrase suggests that one tends to reveal his true feelings under the influence of alcohol. Normally alcohol companies and manufactures target men as their primer customer. The idea behind this project is to bring a woman's touch and softness to the bottles without loosing its presents.

The different fabrics represent different women characteristics, such as cheerful, homey, and dominatrix, and these are equivalent to the different alcohol drinks such as Tequila, Rum, and Vodka; overall there are six different alcohol bottles.

The techniques used in manufacturing these bottles are flock print for the labels (that are made from chiffon fabric), knitted and woven fabrics for the bottles exterior. The bottle itself is made from glass. Printing language: Hebrew.

Design Agency: *Reut Ashkenazy–Graphic Design.* Production Date: *2007.* Designer: *Reut Ashkenazy.* Nationality: *Israel.*

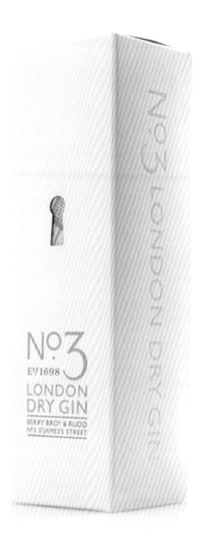

 Berry Bros. & Rudd No.3 London Dry Gin

A complete brand identity – everything from the initial concept to the name and positioning, the die-cast metal key mounted on the front of a bespoke bottle structure and the outer packaging – to offer discerning drinkers the chance to experience "the past, perfected."

Design Agency: *Brandhouse Design*. Production Date: *2010*. Creative Director: *Dave Beard*. Photography: *Brandhouse*. Nationality: *UK*.

 Jekyll & Hyde

Innovative interlocking bottle structures for "the ultimate split personality concoction", a dual component beverage intended to be mixed before consumption. The design intent was to create something very period looking with a dangerous feel.

Design Agency: *Deutsch Design Works.* Production Date: *2007.* Art Director: *Barry Deutsch.* Designer: *Eric Pino.* Client: *Anheuser–Busch InBev.* Nationality: *USA.*

In a Test Specimen

Spirits in a test specimen, the perfect size to taste the spirits. Despite not being any experiment, as in Galicia the "Orujo" spirit is an ancestral tradition.

Design Agency: *Grow_the Design Consultancy*. Production Date: *2009*. Creative Director: *Anna Serra*. Art Director: *Anna Serra*. Designer: *Anna Serra*. Client: *Adegas Ponte da Boga, S.l.* Nationality: *Spain*.

Snälleröds

Snälleröds was established in 1901, but fell into oblivion until Eric Berntson re-launched the brand with a series of organic liquor products. The mission was to establish the history of Snälleröds with a distinct brand platform and also: invent equally eco-friendly design solutions.

The history of Snälleröds is apparent in every aspect of its design and communication with the tagline "a true story" and visual solutions always telling that very story. The packaging design, in some cases, is the first ever of its kind; everything being totally environmentally friendly.

Snälleröds has received a lot of extremely positive media attention. The innovative packaging design and the appealing gift packages have been as important for the buzz as the actual products.

Design Agency: *Neumeister Strategic Design AB.* Production Date: *2009.* Creative Director: *Peter Neumeister.* Designer: *Peter Neumeister / Tobias Andersson.* Client: *Snälleröds.* Nationality: *Sweden.*

Concertum

Inspired in Asian - originated floral motifs. Bold, coloured, different. Fresh and with personality, like D.O. Rías Baixas wine. A bid that will not go unnoticed, either for its striking nature or for the design of its label and capsule.

Design Agency: *(calcco) Comunicación Visual.* Production Date: *2009.* Creative Director: *Sergio Aja.* Designer: *Eduardo del Pozo.* Client: *Bodegas Santiago Ruiz.* Photography: *Sergio Aja.* Nationality: *Spain.*

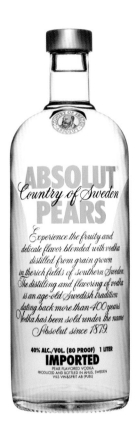

Absolut Pear

Design keywords: V&S Absolut Spirits. Packaging design, naming, Absolut Pears. Worldwide, 2006.

Within extremely strict parameters in terms of form and function, the design was to be unique and innovative, capturing the personality of the product. At the same time it had to be perceived as an obvious member of the Absolut Vodka family. Through the design, the product was to help Absolut to "own" the pear flavour in the market for flavoured vodkas. Absolut was the first to use pear as a vodka flavour.

The starting point for the design solution was the colour signal and the elegant, organic shape of the pear. Using the iconic bottle shape, the design creates an optical illusion of a pear. A traditional shape in a more unconventional way. The design solution is technically efficient, which is important for production.

Design Agency: *BVD*. Production Date: *2006*. Creative Director: *Catrin Vagnemark*. Designer: *Rikard Ahlberg / Bengt Anderung*. Client: *Pernod Ricard, V&S Group*. Nationality: *Sweden*.

Absolut Ruby Red

V&S Absolut Spirits. Packaging design, Absolut Ruby Red. Worldwide, 2005. Within extremely strict parameters in terms of form and function, the design was to be unique and innovative, capturing the personality of the product. At the same time it had to be perceived as an obvious member of the Absolut Vodka family. Through the design, the product was to help Absolut to "own" the ruby grapefruit flavour in the market for flavoured vodkas. Absolut was the first to use ruby grapefruit as a vodka flavour.

The warm red colour comes from the palette of the ruby grapefruit itself. The round, geometric shapes on the outside of the bottle are inspired by the way you cut up and serve the fruit. The technique of printing the warm red shapes using a transparent ink on an etched bottle creates a sense of depth that became the hallmark of the design. The solution is technically efficient, which is important for production.

Design Agency: BVD. Production Date: 2005. Creative Director: Catrin Vagnemark. Designer: Rikard Ahlberg / Bengt Anderung. Client: Pernod Ricard, V&S Group. Nationality: Sweden.

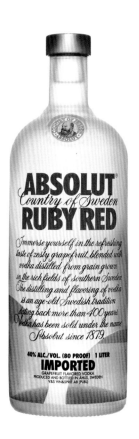

Belvedere Intense Unfiltered 80

BrandOpus created a story around the provenance of the Dankowskie Diamond Rye, and designed a bottle that maintains the Intense equities of metallic on black. The Belvedere tree device depicted in gold draws on the caramel and honey impressions of the vodka, whilst elevating premium cues, whilst the watermark Belvedere palace echoes the window device used across the wider range from the world's most awarded vodka brand.

Design Agency: *BrandOpus.* Production Date: *2010.* Creative Director: *Paul Taylor.* Client: *LVMH.* Nationality: *UK.*

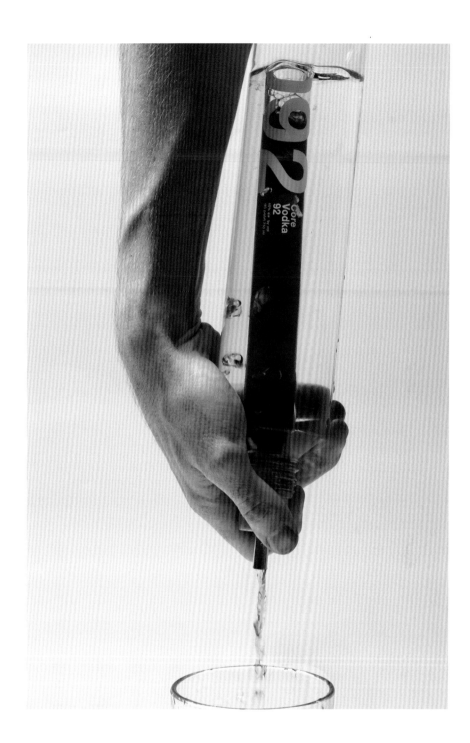

 Core092

A conceptual vodka brand. Using inspiration from nuclear reactors, the goal was to have a two-part bottle that, when poured, would pour a perfectly mixed drink.

Designer: *Jon Patterson*. Photography: *Jon Patterson*. Nationality: *USA*.

Domaine de Canton

After the client launched this French ginger liqueur brand, he realised that it needed some polishing to better reach its target market. The label and marketing collateral lacked the sophisticated French sensibility to convey the spirit of the product, while appealing to women, upscale bartenders, and metro-area drinkers.

So when they invited Mucca to reposition the brand, they responded with an enthusiastic, "Oui!". Beginning with a label redesign, the designers made every part of the packaging and presentation more sophisticated and expressive of the French-Indochinese aesthetic that characterises the origins of the liqueur's recipe. They also worked to communicate the brand story, and its message of high-quality, exotic romanticism throughout all aspects of the brand identity, including advertising, billboards, trade show and instore displays, a website, recipe books, gift packaging, and even groovy little swizzle sticks.

Both the design and the product have garnered rave reviews, and Domaine de Canton has become an internationally successful brand, trumpeted by Oprah and appearing on "Iron Chef". The brand identity has continued to evolve with the rapid growth of the product's market.

Design Agency: *Mucca Design*. Production Date: *2007*. Creative Director: *Matteo Bologna*. Art Director: *Andrea Brown*. Designer: *Andrea Brown / Lauren Sheldon / Ariana DiLibero*. Client: *Domaine de Canton*. Nationality: *USA*.

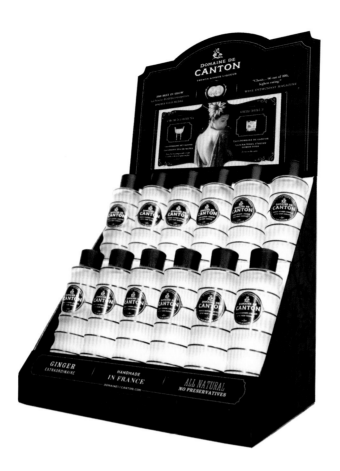

 Belvedere Macerations

Careful to visually balance the purity of Belvedere super premium vodka, while retaining bright characters of the fruit infusions across the maceration family, BrandOpus commissioned bespoke illustrations to capture the distinctive ingredients of each maceration, and present them in a vibrant, modern, illustrative style that forms the heart of the bottle design. The result is a distinctive and recognisable structure.

Design Agency: *BrandOpus*. Production Date: *2008*. Creative Director: *Paul Taylor*.
Client: *LVMH*. Nationality: *UK*.

Porto Wine

It's a premium line of old Soviet porto wines.

Design Agency: *DDH Studio*. Production Date: *2010*. Creative Director: *Nadie Parshina*. Designer: *Nadie Parshina*. Client: *Creative Wine Company*. Nationality: Russia.

Ouzo ZARBANIS

One of the most well - known names in the alcoholic drinks market; this pack's intention was to revisit traditionally used symbols thus to reinvent them creating a fresh, refined image for this product category. Greece as a provenance is evident through the use of the colour cyan and the detail of the miniature church (seen through the glass and the clear liquid inside), reminiscent of the "Greek-style" miniatures on sale in small tourist shops.

Design Agency: *Mousegraphics.* Production Date: *2010.* Creative Director: *Gregory Tsaknakis.* Client: *Zarbanis & Co.* Nationality: *Greece.*

Septiembre Cool Wines

Bodegas Trapiche from Mendoza, Argentina commissioned package design firm
Tridimage to renew the brand image and packaging of their cool wine Septiembre
(September), one of the leaders of the Argentine market. Based on the concept of
"Spring night" the new flower icon builds colourful patterns in each flavour label.

Design Agency: *Tridimage*. Production Date: *2009*. Creative Director: *Adriana
Cortese / Virginia Gines / Hernán Braberman*. Client: *Bodegas Trapiche*.
Nationality: *Argentina*.

Cabo Wabo Tequila:
Blanco Reposado Anejo

Meat and Potatoes was officially named the "agency of record" for Cabo Wabo Tequila in 2009 when the company was sold to SKYY/Campari. First order of business was to re-design the packaging for worldwide manufacturing & distribution, and position the brand as the authentic super-premium rock-n-roll tequila. The previous packaging had three different bottle colours, clear, blue and brown. The blue bottle being the signature of the line. In order to refine the glass for mass production the coloured glass had to be abandoned, but the colour was retained within the labels to help consumers and fans of the tequila make the change to the new look.

The glass shape was refined to the standards of the preceding Cabo Uno packaging. The inset panel is the framework for the wrap-around two-sided label. The label itself is printed with three spot colours, foil stamped, embossed, and laminates to a second acetate label for the inside printing. Each bottle has a different illustration on the inside label.

Its overall boldness has been successful in gaining exposure the brand needed on shelf.

Design Agency: *Meat and Potatoes, Inc.* Production Date: *2009.* Creative Director: *Todd Gallopo / TJ River.* Art Director: *TJ River / Todd Gallopo.* Designer: *TJ River / Todd Gallopo / Danielle Marquez.* Client: *SKYY / Campari.* Photography: *Meat and Potatoes, Inc.* Nationality: *USA.*

Brooklyn Gin

Inspired by the ingenuity of Brooklyn, a sometimes gritty, but always soulful borough, the designers crafted a visual identity for Brooklyn Gin that blends old world craftsmanship with today's artistic, vibrant culture. The bottle structure pays homage to the apothecary origins of gin, reinforcing its place in the new speakeasy, while the medallion label – stamped in metal – celebrates the authentic spirit at the core of the brand.

For the modern mixologist, Brooklyn Gin captures the magic and magnetism of a time and a place where the cocktail is king.

Design Agency: *Spring Design Partners, Inc.* Production Date: *2010.* Creative Director: *Ron Wong.* Designer: *Tet Marti.* Client: *Maverick Spirits.* Photography: *Livio Dimulescu.* Nationality: *USA.*

Antigua Cruz Tequila

Mexico's Tequilera de Arandas company recently chose the Buenos Aires-based Tridimage design firm to redesign Antigua Cruz tequila's structural and graphic packaging for a global audience. The previous squat, square bottle had been used by other tequila brands, which deprived Antigua Cruz differentiation and unique positioning, and the label design was not competitive in the current international tequila market.

Tridimage created a glass bottle structural design with premium personality, standing out from the competition by using sophisticated and expressive resources of high visual impact. The new screen-printed graphics introduced a new icon and logo redesign that conveys the polarity between classicism and modernity.

The angular shape and neo-Gothic font logo convey an accessible premium personality while borrowing design sensibilities from the perfume and cosmetics categories.

Design Agency: *Tridimage*. Production Date: *2010*. Creative Director: *Adriana Cortese / Virginia Gines / Hernán Braberman*. Client: *Tequilera de Arandas*. Photography: *Dany Kamida*. Nationality: *Argentina*.

Diva Maya

Organic tequila brand, Diva Maya donates a
percentage of sales to local Mexican charities which
aid wildlife protection. The brief was to reflect this
without having to write it, while still remaining stylish
and collectible. Each tequila, blanco, reposado and
anejo is represented by an animal, namely turtles,
eagle and jaguar respectively.

Design Agency: *Design by Alpha*. Production Date:
2008. Creative Director: *Anastasia Gerali*. Designer:
Anastasia Gerali. Photography: *Nikos Louka*.
Nationality: *Cyprus*.

 **Russell's Reserve**

It's redesign of the Russell's Reserve premium line of bourbon and rye whiskey.

Design Agency: *Sterling Brands.* Production Date: *2009.* Creative Director: *Debbie Millman / Simon Lince.* Designer: *Irina Ivanova.* Client: *Wild Turkey.* Nationality: *USA.*

Samurai

Another independent non-commercial development by the studio was about an uniquely shaped rice vodka bottle. Its austere outline and the silhouette as if split by a stroke of a samurai sword spectacularly transmit the idea and the ethnic background of the product. The material is high quality glass with décor.

Design Agency: StudioIN. Production Date: 2010. Creative Director: Arthur Schreiber. Designer: Arthur Schreiber. Nationality: Russia.

Bombay Sapphire
Limited Edition

In celebration of the 250-year anniversary of Bombay Sapphire's secret gin recipe, Webb deVlam defined the brand's essence through exclusive packaging design: 350 limited edition hand blown crystal bottles, composed of the finest materials and detailing.

An internal blue optic creates a "bottle within a bottle" effect, signifying the soul of the brand. 3D laser etchings float within the walls of the glass. Garrard's Creative Director, Stephen Webster, conceived the stopper, which features a gold crown encrusted with blue gems. Such intriguing visual effects impart Bombay Sapphire's luxury proposition.

Design Agency: *Webb deVlam*. Production Date: *2010*. Client: *Bacardi*. Nationality: *USA*.

The Macallan 57 in Lalique

Design Bridge created a gift box for the 57 - year - old The Macallan in Lalique inspired The Macallan's third pillar "The Finest Cut". The premium box is both visually interesting and structurally challenging. It reflects the quality of the product inside whilst both protecting and showcasing the precious Lalique decanter.

Design Agency: *Design Bridge*. Production Date: *2009*. Creative Director: *Antonia Hayward*. Designer: *Laurent Robin-Prevallee / Asa Cook*. Client: *Edrington Group*. Nationality: *USA*.

The Macallan 55

Design Bridge incorporated wood, leather and silver into the Macallan 55's packaging – showcasing a new and sophisticated combination of materials for the brand. The result is luxurious, with layers of detail that increase The Macallan's desirability.

Design Agency: *Design Bridge*. Production Date: *2009*. Creative Director: *Antonia Hayward*. Designer: *Laurent Robin–Prevallee, Asa Cook*. Client: *Edrington Group*. Nationality: *UK*.

Karadag Wine

The main idea of a collection is to remind us of the disappearing breeds of animals and birds which live in Karadag. Karadag is a conservancy area on the Pontic sea, in the Crimea. On each bottle described species of an animal or a bird and its short description.

The part of money from wine sale is listed in WWF.

Design Agency: *Nadie Parshina Studio*. Production Date: *2008*. Creative Director: *Nadie Parshina*. Designer: *Nadie Parshina*. Nationality: *Russia*.

Fleur de Lis

Designing the concept of a cognac for women, the designers counted on the elegant modern appearance and the vivid memorable name. One of the most popular heraldic figures, Fleur de Lis (the lily) inspired the designers to create a feminine-shaped bottle. The slightly coquettish fonts emphasise the refined character of the product. The bottle design is also carefully considered. The cork, non-typical for a cognac, allows to effortlessly close and reopen the bottle.

Design Agency: *StudioIN*. Production Date: *2010*. Art Director: *Arthur Schreiber*. Designer: *Arthur Schreiber*. Nationality: *Russia*.

LCBO

A six-pack assortment of the world's finest beers transcends a "battle of the brands" approach to showing all identities, in favour of a starkly bold, distinctive typographical approach.

Design Agency: *Blok Design*. Creative Director: *Vanessa Eckstein*. Designer: *Vanessa Eckstein*. Client: *LCBO*. Nationality: *Canada*.

Label Design
for Mille Plateaux Ginger Beer

Mille Plateaux is a niche and eccentric little ginger beer made by the Dirty Minds
Wine Co. The brief was to design a label that would tell us just that, a label that's
unlike any other ginger beers. With references to a book called Mille Plateaus that
no one will ever get, and the green light to do something a bit different, this is the
result.

Production Date: *2009.* Art Director: *Justin Overell / Monique Kneepkens.*
Designer: *Monique Kneepkens.* Client: *Dirty Minds Wine Co.* Nationality: *Australia,
the Netherlands.*

Samson Beer

Bottle design and branding for New Jersey-based craft brewer Jeff Samson. In the crowded market place of microbrews, a bottle needs to both communicate as well as entertain. The design needs to be clean and uncluttered. And as with all beer packaging, if a little of the brands personality can show through, the better chance it has of connecting with the consumer.

The illustration on the bottle takes the legend of Samson and the Lion and adds a beverage industry twist. These liter bottles are screen printed front and back and packaged in original re-purposed beverage crates.

Design Agency: *Bricks Through Windows.* Production Date: *2010.* Designer: *Sean Flanagan.* Client: *Samson Craft Beers.* Photography: *Brion McCarthy.* Nationality: *USA.*

 Thorsteinn Beer Brand

This beer brand concept was born on a Sunday night at school when the designers were supposed to make a brand for a micro-brewery. The name is traditional Icelandic name that could be loosely translated into "thirsty one".

The concept is to have one beer, 10 different bottle designs by 10 different designers. The design would be changed annually and could be put on beer glasses as well. The designers decided on making versatile design but limit it down to a single colour graphics. The approach was different, but they all shared the same ideology about breaking out of the ordinary and making graphics that aren't exactly typical for beer bottle labelling. The concept also makes the brand a platform for other graphic designers to show off their own design for design's sake.

Production Date: *2010.* Creative Director: *Thorleifur Gunnar Gíslason / Geir Olafsson / Hlynur Ingolfsson.* Designer: *Thorleifur Gunnar Gíslason / Geir Olafsson / Hlynur Ingolfsson.* Photography: *Hellert.* Nationality: *Iceland.*

 ## "Miller Preg-no Non-alcoholic Beer"

The assignment was to design and package a non-alcoholic beer for Miller. The name "Miller Preg-no" came from the idea to target towards pregnant women who like the refreshing taste of beer but don't want the alcohol because of the obvious. Marketed towards pregnant women, it was intended for women to be able to go out and have fun being social without feeling too much out of place.

The contents of the all-natural beer include vitamins and minerals that are healthy for the baby and the mother. It lets the mother feel better about drinking the non - alcoholic beer knowing that it is good for her.

Because this is an exclusive beer, the packaging was meant to be exclusive as well. Under each bottle cap are different baby names that can help the mother decide on a name before the baby is born. They are marked in blue for boy names, pink for girl names, or tan for unisex names. Because it is socially looked down upon to drink alcohol while pregnant, a label underneath the bottle says "100% Non-Alcoholic. Quit Judging." This appears whenever a drink is taken and the bottom of the bottle can be seen.

The exterior packaging explains the bottle caps on the side, while the front explains the beer and its intent. To go along with the theme of the beer, the six-pack is labeled as "sextuplets".

Production Date: *2010*. Creative Director: *Zac Jacobson*. Designer: *Zac Jacobson*. Client: *Miller*. Photography: *Zac Jacobson*. Nationality: *USA*.

🍾 Db Export Limited Edition
🍾 Quart Twin Pack

As part of the re-launch of the Export beer brands, Dow Design was asked to design a limited edition of the original DB Export Beer. Developed in the 1960s by the famous New Zealand brewer Morton Coutts, the objective was to create an authentic story around the origins of DB Export and a credible link to the historic beer while enhancing the brand's masculinity.

Morton Coutts once said "let nothing come between a man and a great beer" and this limited edition pack evokes a bygone era, yet links with the modern DB beer family. The traditional brown card pack conjures up a time when men like Coutts took on the establishment and the government to create a beer that would be a world-class winner. This was a no nonsense time where men got things done.

The beer label itself remains true to the original, with a slight modern twist in the gold label. The original quart bottle size adds to that traditional allure. Along with the limited edition bottle opener, the package becomes a souvenir to remind the owner of the quality and origins of DB Export long after the beer has been drunk.

Design Agency: *Dow Design Ltd.* Production Date: *2010.* Creative Director: *Donna McCort.* Designer: *Will Fletcher.* Client: *DB Breweries.* Photography: *Hellert.* Nationality: *New Zealand.*

Osjecko Pivo (Beer of Osijek)

Osječko Pivo is the brand which, thanks to its rebranding and redesign, united traditional and modern elements. The simple, clean and minimalist design embodies the modern and urban side of its image, while the tradition of the first Croatian beer is shown through the brewery's coat of arms pictured on the packaging.

Design Agency: *Brandoctor*. Production Date: *2009*. Art Director: *Igor Manasteriotti*.
Designer: *Mia Maric*. Client: *Osjecka Pivovara*. Nationality: *Croatia*.

Cuervo Azt

In the year 2010, Mexico celebrated its 200th anniversary as independent country; the Tequila House Co. "Jose Cuervo" inspired by this special date, asked CR84 to develop a special label for a limited number of bottles commemorating this special occasion.

This design is centred over a geometrical pattern depicting one of the most recognised shapes of the ancient world, "the sun stone" (better known as Aztec calendar). The Aztecs were one of the most important civilisations that lived in the region now recognised as Mexico nowadays their symbols are an essential part of the Mexican identity and imaginary.

Design Agency: *CR84*. Production Date: *2010*. Designer: *Cesar Gomez*. Client: *Jose Cuervo (tequila House Co.)* Nationality: *Sweden*.

Session Lager

A conceptual beer study specifically marketed towards snowboarders. Extruded aluminium handles allow easy opening, while the bottles can be worn under the snow jacket, "suicide-bomber" style.

Designer: *Jon Patterson*. Photography: *Jon Patterson*.
Nationality: *USA*.

Kudos Beer

An innovative approach to beer, brewed like an ale filtered like a lager, to create a unique high-end product.

Minimal in approach to appeal to a "London-bar" audience and distinctly different to sell the uniqueness of the beer.

Design Agency: *Ryan Martin Design*. Production Date: *2010*. Designer: *Ryan Martin*. Client: *Green Room Ales / Kudos Beer*. Nationality: *UK*.

Real Mccoy

The brief was to update the brand, increase standout, recall, quality cues and reflect the story of Bill McCoy. Reducing the size of "Real" and increasing the size of "McCoy" created more of a focus on the name and more cut-through on shelf. Textural quality was created by deliberately making the mandatories reflect customs and duty stamps. The design had to be simple, strong and flexible as it was applied to a number of other packages.

Creative Director: *Tony Ibbotson*. Designer: *Tony Ibbotson*. Client: *Diageo*. Photography: *Tony Ibbotson*. Nationality: *Australia*.

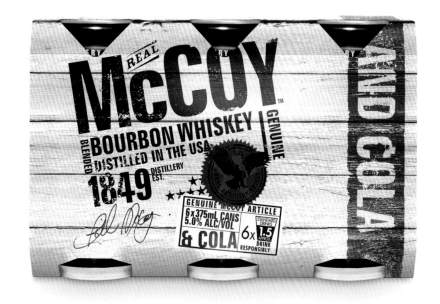

Landshark Lager

When Jimmy Buffett's brand went searchin to launch a refreshing beer in an island state of mind, DDW crafted a legendary rising fin against a sun-yellow background, which anchored LandShark Lager as a proprietary beverage for Margaritaville cafes, retail locations, and LandShark Stadium in Florida.

Design Agency: *Deutsch Design Works*. Production Date: *2008*. Art Director: *Mike Kunisaki*. Designer: *Nancy Andre / Jess Giambroni / Lauren Barr*. Client: *Margaritaville Brewing Co. / Anheuser-Busch InBev*. Nationality: *USA*.

![Swinckels bottle icon] **Swinckels**

The creative idea - the freshness seal - inspired the 3D touchpoints, from the font
through to signage, glassware and pos. The bottle label doubles as a breakable seal
for the cap-a brand experience with a "fresh" perspective.

Design Agency: *Design Bridge.* Production Date: *2007.* Creative Director: *Claire
Parker.* Designer: *Olof ten Hoorn.* Client: *Bavaria.* Nationality: *UK.*

Kirin

In 2007 Lion Nathan established an innovation programme focused on exploring the Kirin brand's opportunity in the Australian market. The outcome was the creation of something quite magical for the brand, a creative outcome defined by the simplicity of authentic Japanese calligraphy designed to embody the unique Kirin brewing process and brand heritage.

Design Agency: *DiDONATO Partners*. Production Date: *2008*. Creative Director: *Tim Wilson*. Designer: *Amber Bonney / Giosuè Prochilo*. Calligraphy: *Junko Azukawa*. Client: *Lion Nathan Australia*. Nationality: *Australia*.

Tooheys Extra Dry 5 Seeds

Launched in 2009, this was an innovation programme that saw the creation of a new product born from the Tooheys family after over 140 years of beer brewing credentials! The Tooheys Extra Dry brand identity and packaging has been designed to take the drinker on a journey of discovery - it evokes a sense of adventure and mystique and breaks traditional category conventions.

Design Agency: *DiDONATO Partners.* Production Date: *2009.* Creative Director: *Damian Kelly.* Designer: *Morice Kastoun.* Client: *Lion Nathan Australia.* Nationality: *Australia.*

Doss Blockos

The creative objective was to capture the brand essence through physical packaging, logo and artwork derived from the story and product concept of Doss Blockos. It needed to reflect the art, music and culture, capture the rawness of getting by on the bare essentials and take inspiration from the arts culture imbedded in the underground squat community of New York during the 1990's.

Design Agency: *Big Dog Creative*. Production Date: *2010*. Creative Director: *Josh Lefers / Stephen Wools*. Designer: *Kane Marevich*. Client: *East 9th Brewing*. Photography: *Conrad Bizjak*. Nationality: *Australia*.

 Beer Bottles

It's the design for a Swedish high quality beer label. The beer is produced in Sweden.

Design Agency: *Edholm Ullenius*. Production Date: *2010*. Creative Director: *Sissi Edholm / Lisa Ullenius*. Designer: *Sissi Edholm / Lisa Ullenius*. Client: *Wicked Wine*. Photography: *Erika Lidén*. Nationality: *Sweden*.

 Brahma Carnava–Limited Edition

It's a special edition for Brahma beer, reflecting the joy and fun of the carnival. In the layout, you can see feathers, masks and dancers, as icons of the event. The sparkles that light makes in the can are an additional ingredient, caused by little silver circles around the silhouettes.

Design Agency: *Pierini Partners.* Production Date: *2011.* Creative Director: *Adrián Pierini.* Designer: *Adrián Pierini.* Client: *Cervecería y Maltería Quilmes.* Nationality: *Argentina.*

🍾 Brahma Chopp Limited Edition
🍾 Argentinean Northeast

It's a special edition of Brahma beer, enhancing the best aspects of the Argentinean Northeast. In its high-impact graphic, a variety of emblematic figures are superimposed in a stylised way. Many can be recognised between the colourful lines, as a woman's smile, a fish, a toucan, showing natural beauties, and the joy and festivities of the people.

Design Agency: *Pierini Partners*. Production Date: *2010*. Creative Director: *Adrián Pierini*. Designer: *Adrián Pierini*. Client: *Cervecería y Maltería Quilmes*. Nationality: *Argentina*.

Back Label

With a very low price point of 5.99 dollar, Back Label competes in the cleanskin wines market. The solution works on two levels, both of which utilise the brand name. As a front label, Back Label appears backwards; however, when the bottle is rotated and the label becomes a back label, the brand name appears correctly.

Design Agency: *Voice*. Production Date: *2009*. Designer: *Anthony de Leo*. Client: *Back Label Wines*. Nationality: *Australia*.

 Massai

Design a commemorative wine bottle and its packaging that represents a particular country. In this case the design was inspired by the African ethnic group Massai located in Kenya.

The tall, thin, dark bottle suited best the designer's way to symbolise the Massai women. The colourful beaded necklace was handmade and used as the main ornamentation, conveying the Massai Tribe's distinctive accessories. As for the logotype, a custom - made typography was developed by the designer. The toughest task was to find a bamboo piece that could fit the bottle inside. Carpentry was needed to remove the bamboos inner fill in order to create a cavity and to make the lid.

Design Agency: *Designbymar*. Production Date: *2006*. Designer: *María del Mar Reyes*. Nationality: *Mexico*.

 JAQK Cellars

JAQK Cellars is a collaboration between Hatch Design founders and a renowned Napa Valley winemaker. Named after the Jack, Ace, Queen, and King in a deck of cards, it is a new wine company dedicated to "play". The packaging of all eight wines in the inaugural offering evoke the allure and sophistication of the world of gaming: High Roller, Soldiers of Fortune (the Jacks), Black Clover (clubs), Pearl Handle (the derringer that tamed the gambling saloons), 22 Black (roulette), Bone Dance (dice), Her Majesty (the Queen), and Charmed (the luckier the better).

Design Agency: *Hatch Design*. Production Date: *2008*. Creative Director: *Katie Jain / Joel Templin*. Designer: *Joel Templin / Katie Jain / Eszter T. Clark / Ryan Meis*. Client: *JAQK Cellars*. Nationality: *USA*.

🍾 Whitegates Winery

This brief was to design an identity and way of packaging wine for a new high - end environmentally conscious winery. The idea is that all the bottles are produced the same to reduce excess manufacturing and just print the tags. If the bottle is returned there is a reduction of the next bottles price.

Design Agency: *James McCarthy*. Production Date: *2010.* Creative Director: *James McCarthy*. Art Director: *James McCarthy*. Designer: *James McCarthy*. Client: *Whitegates Winery*. Photography: *James McCarthy*. Nationality: *UK*.

 Alexandre

Alexandre is a vintage port wine with its own name. The fact that each bottle was signed by hand, gives to it an exclusive character, typical of wines that follow a long maduration process in the bottle.

Design Agency: *Box Design Studio.* Production Date: *2010.* Art Director: *José Fernández.* Designer: *José Fernández / Enrique Raimúndez.* Nationality: *USA.*

Dom Henrique

Dom Henrique is a tawny port wine with a look very closed to this city tradition, where the designers wanted to pay tribute to the most characteristic figure around port wines, and to the traditional way of transporting wine in a boat called "rabelo" through the waters of the Duero River.

Design Agency: *Box Design Studio*. Production Date: *2010*. Art Direction: *José Fernández*. Designer: *José Fernández / Enrique Raimúndez*. Nationality: *USA*.

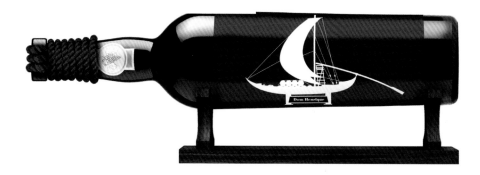

Fire Road

The designers re-design an existing range of labels creating a more simplified and contemporary solution. The labels' origins are based on a famous fire in the Marlborough region that was bravely fought by local residents on a street now known as Fireroad. The designs needed to be bold, impactfull and driven by colour and story. There are currently three wines in the series but the designs must allow for additions to be added over the coming years.

Production Date: *2010*. Creative Director: *Tony Ibbotson*. Designer: *Mayra Monobe*. Nationality: *Australia*.

 Marlborough Sun

The design is to create a new series of wine labels from scratch. This is to include naming, identity and label design. The name and label needed to take advantage of the high profile of Marlborough wines across the globe. It needed to have a clear point of difference from other labels, needed to standout on shelf, have a sense of humour and most importantly create a talking point. If there was a way that the labels could reinvent themselves each year this would also be an advantage as the grapes were specifically selected for each variety and need to display individual characteristics.

Creative Director: *Tony Ibbotson.* Designer: *Andi Yanto.* Client: *Marlborough Valley Wines.* Nationality: *Australia.*

The Wine Society

The Wine Society wanted to upgrade its labels from something that was quite
generic to something that added a little more value. The Society is competing
agains many different wineryies and it was important that the labels had good
standout, reflected the quality and helped beging to tell the WS story. The labels
needed to work across three tiers, a value range, a mid range and a more premium
high - end range. There were over 30 different labels in the whole series so they
needed to feel like a group but also stand alone in their tier.

One of the most telling aspects of the society is how to dress and what to wear. These
labels have beed designed to firstly reflect and re-enforce the idea of "Society" but
also create individual personality and style for each wine. The tie was chosen as the
main visual link as it talked to the idea of a society or a group and a standard. A full
neck tie is used for the value tier and a bow tie is used for the premium and reserve
tier. Each tie has a change of colour and image for each wine.

Creative Director: *Tony Ibbotson*. Designer: *Tony Ibbotson*. Client: *The Wine
Society*. Nationality: *Australia*.

Wishbone

The design is to create a simple and distinctive wine label for the Wishbone brand out of wine out of Marlborough in New Zealand. It is a mainstream wine that needed to be remembered from the 1000's of labels on shelves throughout the world.

The label is simple and clean. Two wishbones form a large W in the centre of the label; this creates a unique focal point and is memorable. A special adhesive label tear section is placed into the front side that can be removed–thus breaking the wishbone; under this label the consumer is encouraged to keep the tab, make another wish and with a bit of luck find another bottle.

Creative Director: *Tony Ibbotson*. Designer: *Mayra Monobe*. Client: *The Creative Method*. Nationality: *Australia*.

Blossa 10

Blossa annual edition is an important member of the Blossa family. It is launched every year with a new flavour and design. The aim of the vintage mulled wine is to generate awareness of Blossa ahead of the mulled wine season and drive sales across the whole range. The design needs to capture the essence of the year's flavour and be unique and alluring.

The solution was a bottle that was shorter and rounder than other Blossa products. The shape of the bottle is kept from year to year, with the colours and typography changing to reflect that particular year's design and flavour. This year's flavour is saffron and the bottle's colour is gold. Gold is an iconic colour that reflects the festive nature of Christmas as well as the taste: saffron with its golden colour is one of the most exclusive of all the spices. The Roman X is used as a symbol for the number 10, but is also a hint at the English X-mas.

Designer Agency: *BVD*. Production Date: *2003–2010*. Design Director: *Catrin Vagnemark / Susanna Nygren Barrett*. Designer: *Sofia Ekvall*. Client: *Pernod Ricard Nordic, V&S Group*. Nationality: *Sweden*.

🍾 Blossa Lingonberry
🍾 and Blossa Orange Light Mulled Wine

The challenge was to further develop Blossa following the successes of their annual
edition mulled wine and create an innovative light mulled wine in the same spirit,
in order to break new ground in consumers' daily shopping.

The solution was to create bottles with an elegant silhouette and graphic expression
which makes them worthy representatives on any drinks tray, and they can also be
purchased in normal food stores. The shape differentiates itself from others in the
hectic environment of the food market industry and ensures the mulled wine is easy
to find, easy to understand and easy to love.

Design Agency: *BVD*. Production Date: *2009*. Creative Director: *Catrin Vagnemark*.
Design Director: *Susanna Nygren Barrett*. Art Director: *Rikard Ahlberg*. Designer:
Mia Heijkenskjöld / Johan Andersson. Client: *Pernod Ricard, V&S Group*.
Nationality: *Sweden*.

Nocturnalis

Designer Marcel Buerkle developed this red and white wine range with a black & white, day & night, sun & moon concept with astrological symbols in a symbolic solar system. The number 24365 stands for 24 hours a day, 365 days a year. The "D" and "N" on the labels will be embossed and the boxes will have a check UV varnished pattern. The concept and elegant design makes for great shelf impact.

To some wine lovers, the difference between white and red wines is one of night and day. Designer Marcel Buerkle created a series of packaging for two wines, a Cabernet Sauvignon and a Sauvignon Blanc, that represent the dynamic nature of the fermented grape. His Nocturnalis and Durinalis wine packaging designs are inspired by the moon and the sun and the movement of the earth between them. Their courses throughout the skies are documented on these labels, giving a starry sense of wonder for what awaits those who pop these corks.

Design Agency: *Circum Punkt Design*. Production Date: *2011*. Designer: *Marcel Buerkle*. Nationality: *South Africa*.

Yellow+Blue Wines

Yellow+Blue, when you mix the two together, you get green - as in environmentally conscious, forward thinking and committed to positive change.

The two interlocking circles represent: The elements sun, water and earth. Unified the letterforms become the Y+B mark.

The designers developed packaging that tells the Y+B story. A quality wine made by artisans and signed by the Founder & President. Wine descriptors and factoids wrap around the eco-friendly carton. The type grows up vertically to create visual impact. Re-Branding included Logo, Packaging, POP, Marketing & Promotional Materials, Corporate Stationary, T shirts and Web Site.

Design Agency: *Spear Design Group*. Production Date: *2010*. Creative Director: *Fiona Spear*. Designer: *Fiona Spear*. Client: *J. Soif, Inc*. Photography: *Geoff Spear*. Nationality: *USA*.

Good Wine Company

The designers were approached by the Good Wine Company who wanted a completely new concept to their wine bottle designs. The client asked the designers to rebrand their new range of organic, and wanted a fresh, clean graphic to reflect the company's organic and natural ethos. The designers also designed and produced exclusive box packing, made from 100% recycled stock to reinforce the sustainable nature of the product and the company.

Design Agency: *ilovedust*. Production Date: *2010*. Nationality: *UK*.

 °n Italian Wine

After becoming very interested in wine, the designers designed these conceptual bottles based on the famous wine regions of Italy, while studying in Rome. The wine labels are based on the longitudes of Italy and its famous wine regions. Depending on the degrees north, the wine region was associated with a numerical logo and topographic map of its location in the country.

Design Agency: *Rob Schellenberg*. Production Date: *2009*. Designer: *Rob Schellenberg*. Photography: *Rob Schellenberg*. Nationality: *USA*.

Sunboom Wine

The main idea that grapes for this wine grow in very solar district.

Wine has absorbed solar beams that its taste became similar to a sunstroke.

Manufacturers of this wine have invited famous writers to try wine and describe their sensations and thoughts. All their notes have been transferred on bottles without changes.

Design Agency: *Nadie Parshina Studio*. Production Date: *2008*. Designer: *Nadie Parshina*. Nationality: *Russia*.

Paul Sapin

When Paul Sapin launched their series of wine, white, red and rosé, in PET-bottles the awaited success did not occur – although reviews were good. What was the problem?

Neumeister was approached to take a look at the packaging design.

"Easy to go", is the main idea. Classic design with a modern approach. Old meets new, in the same way as the product; traditional French wine, produced in a traditional way, but with a whole new packaging concept. And the twisted label as an eye cather.

Design Agency: *Neumeister Strategic Design AB.* Production Date: *2010.* Designer: *Peter Neumeister / Tobias Andersson.* Client: *NIGABc.* Nationality: *USA.*

Pioneer Block Packaging

A unique hand - crafted series of wine labels to reflect a hand - crafted pioneering
nature used in the grape selection and winemaking.

The Saint Clair Pioneer Block labels are an experimental selection of premium
wines. A series of unique wine labels are created showing a "pioneering" spirit,
hand - crafted influence, history and individual personality. The solution is a series
of handmade typographic stamps placed onto a natural colour serrated stock. A
different stamp placed in a different position denotes the various varieties. Each type
layout is finalised and a rubber stamp is made; this is then inked, stamped, scanned
and placed back onto the final label. The Pioneer Block writing is hand generated
by brush and scanned into the final artwork.

Design Agency: *The Creative Method*. Production Date: *2006*. Creative Director:
Tony Ibbotson. Art Director: *Tony Ibbotson*. Designer: *Tony Ibbotson*. Client: *Saint
Clair Family Estate*. Nationality: *Australia*.

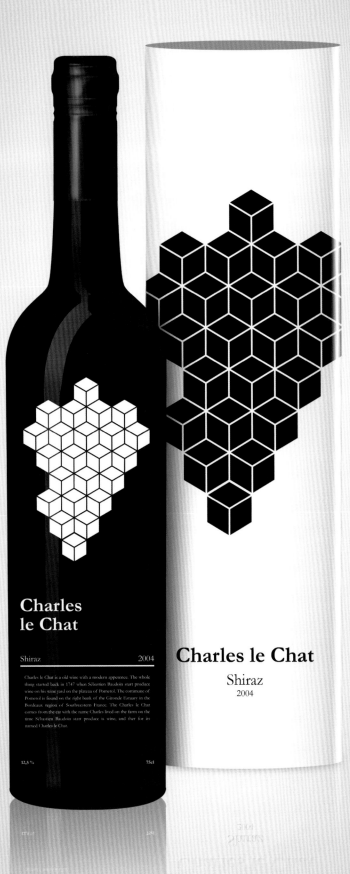

 Charles le Chat

The brief was to make an expensive premium wine.
The idea was to make a modern and simple label
instead of a traditional classic label design. The cubes
symbolised wine grapes to get a modern feeling. The
designer also made a tin can to go with the bottle to
get that luxury feeling.

Production Date: *2010*. Designer: *Victor Eide*.
Photography: *Victor Eide*. Nationality: *Sweden*.

**Charles
le Chat**

Shiraz   2004

Charles le Chat is a old wine with a modern apperence. The whole
thing started back in 1747 when Sebastien Baudoin start produce
wine on his wine yard on the plateau of Pomerol. The commune of
Pomerol is found on the right bank of the Gironde Estuary in the
Bordeaux region of Southwestern France. The Charles le Chat
comes from the cat with the name Charles lived on the farm on the
wine Sebastien Baudoin start produce is wine, and ther for its
named Charles le Chat.

12,5 %   75cl

Charles le Chat
Shiraz
2004

🍾 Ciulla 2008 Holiday Wine Bottle:
🍾 Self Promotion...la La La

The wine label design combines festive graphics and typography along with wordplay to extend holiday wishes to the valued clients and partners. The CIULLA "brand name" becomes an extension of the holiday greeting as a widely known holiday carol's refrain: "Fa la la la la la la la la" changes to "CIULLA La La La" resulting in a bottle of holiday cheer.

Design Agency: *CIULLA ASSOC*. Production Date: *2008*. Creative Director: *Sam J. Ciulla*. Designer: *Shelley Scheer*. Client: *CIULLA ASSOC self promotion*. Nationality: *USA*.

Ciulla 2009 Holiday Wine Bottle:
Self Promotion...wreath

The unique wreath illustration made up of a fine filigree pattern conjures up the lightness and delicate nature of fresh fallen snow or frost on window. The Ciulla brand mark is centred in the wreath with "Salute" positioned below. The brand mark is based on an ancient mythological symbol representing the region of Sicily and "Salute" is the Italian toast for health and well being. Extending holiday greetings to the clients in a most Italian way... with a bottle of wine!

Design Agency: CIULLA ASSOC. Production Date: 2008. Creative Director: Sam J. Ciulla. Designer: Shelley Scheer. Client: CIULLA ASSOC self promotion. Nationality: USA.

 **Fritz Muller**

Fritz Müller - the name is a cheeky referral to what the bottle contains: a sparkling wine (frizzante) made from Müller-Thurgau grapes.

Famous for faceless bulk commodities, this traditional German grape doesn't exactly excite wine connoisseurs. But the designers have rediscovered its best attributes: refreshing fruit and lightness. Well-dressed at a fair price, "Fritz" stands for good, honest, drinking pleasure.

The label contributes to the product's success thanks to its high recognition value. It expresses the designers' philosophy of returning to the authentic quality of regional products, to the roots of German culture and aesthetics in a light and humorous way.

The name and the design unite to form a memorable and incisive brand profile.

Design Agency: *Schmidt / Thurner / Von Keisenberg Büro Für Visuelle*. Production Date: *2010*. Creative Director: *Timo Thurner*. Designer: *Timo Thurner*. Client: *Fritz Müller verperlt GmbH*. Photography: *Anja Prestel*. Nationality: *Germany*.

Malondro Wines

Malondro Wines its a client based in Spain. The project is a redesign of the brand in order to make it more competive in the world of winery. The designers maintained the logo and built the main idea of the product and where it comes from. The main idea of the project was to let the wine express itself. The designers did the illustrations with actual wine and after a digital process included them on the tags. There are two main divisions: the younger and the old wine. The younger wines will be Xabec, Besllum and Latria. The type of illustration is contemporary and appealing to a younger audiences. The old wines (Malondro Blanc, Red and Coelum) illustrates places where the wine it produced. The Winery its really small and the designers wanted to let the place and the origin be one of the main elements of this project.

Design Agency: *Gworkshop*. Production Date: *2010*. Creative Director: *José Luis García Eguiguren*. Designer: *José Luis García Eguiguren*. Client: *Malondro*. Nationality: *Spain*.

Dashe Cellars Wine

It is an imagined brand redesign for Dashe Cellars began with their distinctive label. Stylistically the monkey and fish represent husband and wife winemaking team creating complex wines from top vineyards throughout Sonoma county. While the design vision combined elegance with playfulness, the final illustration helped to elevate the brand and preserve the story behind their wines.

Production Date: *2010.* Designer: *Jenny Pan.* Illustrator: *Richard Perez.* Client: *Academic.* Photography: *Jenny Pan.* Nationality: *USA.*

Angelini Design
Christmas Limited Edition 2010

Black, bright silver and copper red. Matt coated paper with a textured feel and metallic colours for three limited edition labels dedicated to wines brimming with character by a young and talented producer. The fresh Barbera, the generous Nebbiolo and the more aristocratic Barolo are clad with a wise play of "custom typography". Pure geometric lettering on vertical labels with a bold vintage décor effect and a vaguely retro charm. An exercise of customized typography design that rewrites and assembles the letters one on top of the other to build a consistent system of symbols which markedly emphasises the bold flavour of each wine. Each one different, yet all united by the same force and efficacy of communication. Angelini Design picked Simone Scaletta's wines to celebrate Christmas with its customers with the thrilling natural vitality of its fine wines from the soft Langa hill slopes.

Design Agency: *Angelini Design*. Production Date: *2010*. Creative Director: *Andrea Indini*. Designer: *Andrea Indini*. Client: *Simone Scaletta - Angelini Design*. Nationality: *Italy*.

Women' Secret Sun Care Products

Just in time for summer, Women' Secret has launched a line of sun care products. An extension of the label's w'eau, the line features three products: sun lotion, after-sun cream, and facial sun cream. The designers have designed the packaging for the set, using clear, minimal graphics and color so that nothing gets in the way of your rays.

Design Agency: *Basedesign*. Production Date: *2010*. Client: *Women' Secret*. Nationality: *Spain*.

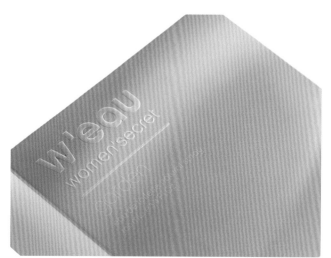

Amala

Amala is a new line of organic skincare products designed primarily for spas, salons and high-end department stores. Liska worked with Amala to define the brand and design everything that touched the distribution and end consumer. From literature to environment-friendly packaging to training materials, Liska carefully controlled every design aspect to establish the Amala brand experience

Design Agency: *Liska+Associates*. Production Date: *2008*. Creative Director: *Tanya Quick*. Designer: *Jenn Cash*. Client: *Amala*. Nationality: *USA*.

amala

rejuvenate
cocoa bean

treatment oil

30ml / 1.0 fl oz

amala

rejuvenate
cocoa bean

treatment oil

amala

purify
blue lotus

purifying
clay mask

50 ml / 1.7 fl oz

amala

purify
blue lotus

purifying
clay mask

amala

hydrate
jasmine

hydrating
toner

100 ml / 3.4 fl oz

amala

hydrate
jasmine

hydrating
toner

amala

detoxify
myrtle

detoxifying
bath crystals

200 g / 7.1 oz net wt

amala

detoxify
myrtle
detoxifying
bath crystals

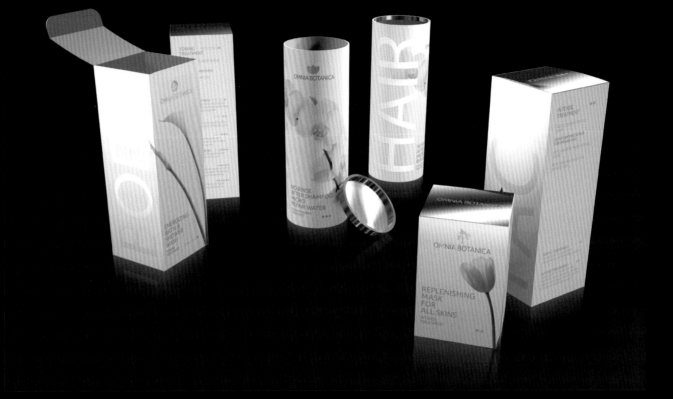

 Omnia Botanica

Omnia Botanica is an Italian beautz brand that looked for talented designers on BOOTB for a new packaging and ID. This was the submission for the range of products with a nature flavour.

Design Agency: *Bürocratik Design*. Production Date: *2008*. Creative Director: *Adriano Esteves*. Art Director:*Adriano Esteves*. Designer: *Adriano Esteves / Ana Camacho*. Client: *Omnia Botanica*. Nationality: *Italy*.

Sanitas Skincare

Sanitas was looking for a way to have their pharmacist-created product line stand out in the forest of tubes, jars and bottles that populate the women's skincare category. At the same time, they wanted the packaging to convey the core attributes that lie at the heart of their biogenic products: clean, healthy, fresh (without being trendy), and clinical (but not sterile).

Design Agency: *Hatch Design*. Production Date: *2009*. Creative Director: *Katie Jain / Joel Templin*. Designer: *Nancy Hsieh*. Client: *Sanitas Skincare*. Nationality: *USA*.

 Barbasol Restyling

This project guideline was to re-style the popular American barbasol in order to introduce it to the European market. The designer focused on utilising the basic form that they have been using for years, the barber shop pole (stripes). The aggressive diagonal line that divides the stripes suggest a mix between the shaving cream and the fragance. Also it reffers to the razor blades on the surface of the skin cutting through the beard. The way the lines drive all the way up and down on the sides makes a perfect simulation of the shaving cream mixing and getting out of the can. The form of the can (cap & bottom) and the shape of the stripes live in perfect armony. The smaller type makes it look more sophisticated and kind of tech.

Design Agency: *Gworkshop*. Production Date: *2009*. Creative Director: *José Luis García Eguiguren*. Designer: *José Luis García Eguiguren*. Client: *Barbasol*. Nationality: *Spain*.

Penhaligon's Sartorial

Capturing the essence of a Savile Row tailor's shop: the thread device weaves together the traditional and the contemporary, providing an angular, masculine expression.

The paper stock utilises cotton fibres to give a real tactile, authentic finish.

Design Agency: *Jones Knowles Ritchie.* Production Date: *2010.* Designer: *Jones Knowles Ritchie.* Client: *Penhaligon's.* Photography: *Peter Thiedeke.* Nationality: *England.*

 Bath and Body Works
Signature Collection P.S. I Love You

The designers create graphics for a modern rose - scented body care line.
Youthful and sophisticated acrylic on canvas heart illustration in reds and blues.
Hand painted graphics and type inspired by handwritten love notes.

Design Agency: *BUREAU–TM.* Production Date: *2010.* Creative Director: *Tommy Everett / Michael Vadino.* Client: *LIMITED BRANDS.* Photography: *Jen Campbell Photography.* Nationality: *USA.*

 Macadamia

The designers set out to create a look for the line that was "modern natural". They wanted to avoid the stereotypical natural, organic aesthetic that all natural-type products seem to gravitate to. These needed to stand out and make you fall in love with them.

The designers felt that a shrink sleeve would give them a lot of creative freedom but the challenge was that these are high-end, expensive professional hair care products and needed to look the part. They needed to find a way to use shrink sleeves in a way that didn't say "supermarket vitamin water". They pulled it off with the use of matte coating combined with spot varnish plus six spot colours. The oil has a clear window knocked out of the art to accentuate the glass and give them a glimpse at the oil inside.

Design Agency: *Version–X Design*. Production Date: *2009*. Creative Director: *Chris Fasan*. Designer: *Chris Fasan / Adam Stoddard*. Client: *Macadamia Natural Oil*. Nationality: *USA*.

 **Aveda Men**

A leader in the world of natural hair and body care, Aveda saw the opportunity to introduce a new line designed specifically for men. Inspired by science, new formulas were created to address unique hair care needs of modern men and in so doing, tap into a huge market potential.

Design Agency: *Duffy & Partners*. Production Date: *2007*. Creative Director: *Dan Olson*. Designer: *Joseph Duffy*. Client: *Aveda*. Nationality: *USA*.

 Innisfree

Innisfree was looking for help in designing a new packaging programme to better reflect the simple beauty of its products' natural offerings. The brand was looking for a greater sense of youthful energy, smart messaging architecture and a more consistent presentation overall. A simple illustration style was created to deliver a sense of energy and a bolder shelf presence. While a colour framework was developed for the continued growth of the brand and to enhance the shopping experience for consumers.

Design Agency: *Duffy & Partners.* Production Date: *2010.* Creative Director: *Joe Duffy.* Designer: *Joseph Duffy.* Client: *Amore–Pacific.* Nationality: *USA.*

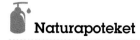 **Naturapoteket**

The packaging failed to communicate Naturapoteket's new core values of "trust", "knowledge", "modernity" and "increased wellbeing". The products needed to be put in the spotlight and made more modern, active and clear. Naturapotektet's products were presented under a separate brand, Royal, without any direct link to Naturapoteket.

The solution was a clear, new graphic identity, with all 160 products carrying Naturapoteket's name now well coordinated, creating a coherent whole and having a uniform tone communicating a younger, more modern and more lively brand.

The products are colour-coded to make it easy for customers to find and choose the right product. The communication on the products is clear, quick and easy.

Design Agency: BVD. Production Date: 1999–2001. Creative Direction: Susanna Nygren Barrett / Catrin Vagnemark. Designer: Kina Giesenfeld / Bengt Anderung. Client: Naturapoteket. Nationality: Sweden.

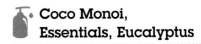

Coco Monoi, Essentials, Eucalyptus

After two decades of success, Thymes needed to reinvent itself to maintain leadership in a cluttered category. Design efforts began with positioning and brand identity work and extended through marketing materials and across a product line of over 20 collections.

A fresh look and new product offerings spurred reinvigorated interest in the Thymes' belief that there is an art to living beautifully, through the even the most essential and simple tasks of daily bathing and homekeeping.

Design Agency: *Duffy & Partners.* Production Date: *2003.* Creative Director: *Dan Olson.* Designer: *Ken Sakurai / Candice Leick.* Client: *Thymes.* Nationality: *USA.*

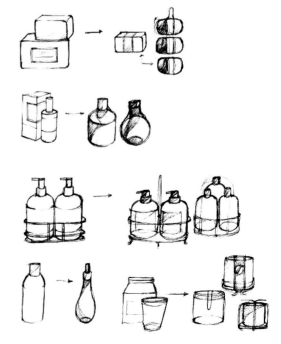

Urban by Levis

For this assignment, the designers had to design a line of bath and body products for an existing brand that has the potential to extend its system into bath and body products. The designer decided to go with Levis. The objective was to create a new brand identity and make it more unique, contemporary and aesthetically appealing to a younger and fresher audience. The design adjectives he decided to incorporate were : vintage, authentic, rugged and stylish. The designer feels that these adjectives are very suitable to the bath and body line, as well as Levi's currently. The target audience he chose for this line were women between the ages of 18 to 25. The labels are stainless steel plates with all the type engraved on it. This he felt added a nice touch of authenticity and toughness and the old apothecary bottles he chose to push forward the idea of vintage.

Production Date: *2010*. Designer: *Harshyla Singh.*
Photography: *Celeste Kacesi Lim.* Nationality: *India.*

 Deli Bodi

"A new spa and home living product with tag line".
Living slowly mainly target to urban people. The
designers wanted the main target to slowdown in
hectic urban lifestyle and enjoy life around them.
All patterns were created from basic computer
ornament giving the idea that everything can become
joyful.

Design Agency: *Default Bangkok*. Production Date:
2010. Designer: *Rapeeparn Kitnichee*. Nationality:
USA.

Face 2 Face

Face to Face is a skin & aesthetic centre in PhEnglandet, Thailand with cutting - edge FDA-approved products. The package was created with clean, simple typography to communicate with the main target audience which is the Western traveller.

Design Agency: *Default Bangkok*. Production Date: *2008*. Designer: *Akarit Leeyavanich / Sataporn Nuallaong*. Nationality: *USA*.

 Estelle & Thild

Estelle & Thild started as an ecological and exclusive body care series for babies and children. The products are the result of two years of development work that was performed in consultation with pediatricians, toxicologists and dermatologists.
Estelle & Thild provides the first Ecocert certified range of baby care products to the Swedish market.

A characteristic feature of our times is that many people value ecological and natural products, whether they are for clothes, food or skin care. Most people are especially anxious to provide their children with the very best in terms of health.

The design concept, which communicates the company's soft and natural values, was subsequently produced. Parents constitute the primary target group that should be attracted by packaging and products. It should be clear to the consumer that the products are created for babies and children.

A playful yet clean "Scandinavian" manner was applied to the packaging to appeal to eco - conscious parents with young children. The pattern of avocado leaves reappears throughout the Estelle & Thild profile, not only on the packages, as avocado oil is one of the most frequently used ingredients in the range. The pattern also symbolises the natural origin of the products. The products are differentiated from each other by the mild pastel colours, often associated with children's products.

Design Agency: *Dolhem Design*. Production Date: *2009*. Designer: *Christophe Dolhem / Anna Lindelöw*. Client: *Estelle & Thild*. Nationality: *Sweden*.

lavanta
bitki yağı

nua spa

lavender
essential oil

30 ml

Nua Spa

Nua Spa, corporate identity and packaging design was a graduation project. Nua Spa had taken the name from Richmond Hotel's Nua Wellness & Spa. However, only name used as Nua Spa, designs and general structure of the company are completely re-established. The company the designer created producing completely natural products from herbal formulas. Not testing on animals, respectful to the human life, creatures within the world and nature. It was important that the design of these products would be outstanding and different from the products in market already. All efforts were made to create a product line which is quality, attractive and natural (eco-friendly). As a result, the designer decided to use watercolour and textured paper in designs. which are great tools to give naturalness. Two colours used maximum and a single typeface family.

Production Date: *2009*. Designer: *Merve Selvi*. Nationality: *Poland*.

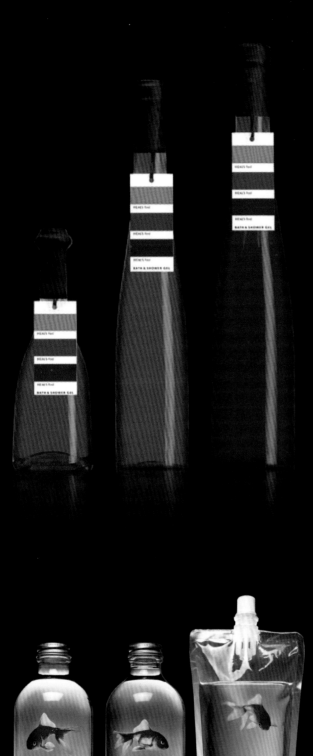

Heals Bathroom

The designers have created "must have" packaging that looked gorgeous on the bathroom shelf.

Design Agency: *Brandhouse Design*. Production Date: *2008*. Creative Director: *Dave Beard*. Photography: *Brandhouse*. Nationality: *UK*.

Kinvara Smoked Salmon
Packaging Design – Pates

The design agency, burst* designed an extension to the Kinvara Smoked Salmon Range, branding a new range of Smoked Salmon Patés. The design had to include a tamper evident device. Colour - changing background was used to differentiate the flavours.

Design Agency: *burst*. Production Date: *2009*. Creative Director: *Kasia Rust.*
Designer: *Kasia Rust.* Client: *Kinvara Smoked Salmon.* Nationality: *Ireland.*

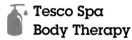
The objective was to create a stand-alone brand including logo, name and identity that could be applied across four product offerings: serenity, vitality, detox and smooth and svelte. R Design created a strong brand where both colour and illustration change but are all recognised as part of a whole.

Creative Director: *David Richmond*. Designer: *Iain Dobson / Sarah Bustin*. Client: *Tesco*. Nationality: *UK*.

232

233

Soap & Glory for Men

How do you get men to have fun while they shave and lather? Soap & Glory for Men has all the sass of the ladies line but with a rock 'n roll edge inspired by great British icons such as The Who and The Beatles. It utilises ridiculously tongue-in-cheek humour, rock 'n roll type models photographed with British flair, bold product descriptors, strong typography and a signature British colour palette. Sexy "babe magnet", Eau Man Eau de Toilette spray, has a more modern and sophisticated design approach than its "brother" base line products so that it may compete with higher end and expensive male lifestyle fragrances on the market.

Designer Agency: *Biggs&Co*. Production Date: *2009–2011*. Designer: *Alli Truch/ Kim Biggs*. Client: *Soap & Glory Cosmetics*. Photography: *Jake Chessum*. Nationality: USA.

Babe Pediatrica

Design of bottles and graphic for pediatric range.
Illustrations by Juan Antón.

Design Agency: *Lavernia & Cienfuegos*. Production
Date: *2008*. Designer: *Lavernia & Cienfuegos*. Client:
Babé. Nationality: *Spain*.

 Solcare

Design of bottle and graphics for sun cream.

Design of the bottles and graphics of a sun cream sold by the distribution chain MERCADONA. The shapes of the bottles are inspired by the stones of the beaches. The range has a total of 40 products.

Designer Agency: *Lavernia & Cienfuegos*. Production Date: *2008*. Designer: *Lavernia & Cienfuegos*. Client: *SRNB Laboratories*. Nationality: *Spain*.

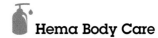

Hema Body Care

Hema is a Dutch retail organisation with stores in the Netherlands, Belgium, Luxemburg, France and Germany. Customer-friendly and with a unique profile, HEMA distinguishes itself from other retailers by selling its own brand. Planeta Design was given the task to re-design their package in their "Better" segment within Body Care.

The challenges were to communicate the brand as low price yet with high quality on the international market and to take an already established brand into the international market without interfering with their high recognition on the national market. The result of the cooperation led to a basic and colourful concept with a clear and customer-friendly communication so that the customer easily knows what the products do for you. The concept is fitting perfectly in the company's strategy to surprise customers with convenient, practical, attractive products of good quality.

Design Agency: *Planeta Design*. Production Date: *2011*. Creative Director: *Sandra Planeta*. Designer: *Magnus Linehag*. Client: *HEMA*. Photography: *Kristofer Samuelsson*. Nationality: *Sweden*.

skintuary

Sanitizing
& Moisturizing
Hand Cream

Crème à main
antiseptique
& hydratante

4-Hour Protection
Protection 4 heures

Kills 99.9% of germs
Tue 99.9% des germes

Alcohol and triclosan free
Sans alcool, sans triclosan

5 FI OZ/140 ML

ingredients

Vitamin E,
Avocado Oil,
Jojoba Oil &
Grape Seed Oil
Protects &
moisturizes hands
Note: Unscented

Vitamine E,
huile d'avocat,
huile de jojoba
et huile de pépin
de raisin
Protège et hydrate
les mains
Note: Non-parfumé

 **Skintuary**

Mookai was mandated to propose branding concepts for a new sanitising hand cream being introduced on the market. The cream's breakthrough formula acts as a shield for hands, protecting them from germs for up to four hours while providing moisture. The product's distribution at an upscale cosmetic retailer meant that it had to appeal to women and reflect cleanliness while still feeling elegant. Through development of product name "Skintuary" and packaging design, Mookai was able to achieve a benefit-oriented, feminine and upscale proposed final product.

Designer Agency: *Mookai Communications*. Production Date: *2010*. Creative Direction: *Lori von Sychowski*. Art Direction: *Lori von Sychowski*. Designer: *Tanya Duffy*. Nationality: *Canada*.

 826 Valencia Pirate Supply Store

Office collaborated with 826 Valencia, a nonprofit tutoring centre for youth, to reinvigorate its pirate supply storefront. The designers developed the store's new identity, and conceptualised and developed nearly 50 new products. "Office has produced some of the most ravishing and funny buccaneer supplies yet known to man," said Dave Eggers, 826 Valencia founder and McSweeney's editor. Reflecting the store's wildly imaginative experience, the products represent 826's mission to support creative expression. All proceeds directly benefit 826 Valencia's writing programmes.

Design Agency: *Office*. Production Date: *2008*. Creative Director: *Jason Schulte / Jill Robertson*. Designer: *Jason Schulte / Rob Alexander / Will Ecke, Gaelyn Jenkins / Jeff Bucholtz*. Writers: *Dave Eggers / Lisa Pemrick / Jon Adams / Anna Ura / Dan Weiss / Jennifer Traig*. Client: *826 Valencia*. Photography: *Vanessa Chu*. Nationality: *USA*.

 CalBen

With a great product and message CalBen has been progressing forward for decades; however, their appearance hasn't transitioned. This family - run business was brought into the present with a strong retail presence, while still maintaining the sense of company longevity, history and quality. This is the entirely new range of consumer packaging.

Designer Agency: *WOND3R*. Production Date: *2010*. Creative Direction: *Aaron Ricchio*. Designer: *Aaron Ricchio*. Client: *Michael Gerbino*. Photography: *Angeloh Christian*. Nationality: *USA*.

 ## Jason Markk 4 Oz. Premium Sneaker Solution Set

Jason Markk offers a smaller, more affordable version of their popular premium sneaker cleaning kit.

In addition to its smaller, more compact size, the exterior of JM's trademark sneaker box packaging has been completely redone - this time paying homage to the game of basketball. After all, sneakers and basketball go hand-in-hand. The kit's basketball motif is printed in metallic silver and is treated with a clear, raised UV that gives the ball design actual texture that you can see and feel.

The new kit includes a four ounce bottle of Original Premium Sneaker Solution, a slightly smaller, handcrafted wood brush with an oversized JM bubble icon logo laser etched into the handle, an informative FAQs card, and retails for 15 dollars.

Design Agency: *Chhun Tang Visual Communications*. Production Date: *2010*. Designer: *Chun Tang / April Larivee*. Client: *Jason Markk*. Nationality: *USA*.

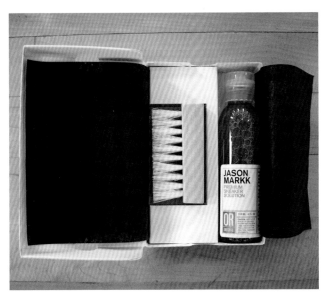

Neil George Hair Care:
Pure Shot Treatment Spray

Creating a branded identity using classic Bodoni allowed the designers to create clean, smart packaging when it came to each individual product in this high-end hair care line. The Pure Shot packaging was created to house five individual oil treatments. Its presentation and packaging were just as important and its function, elegance with superior quality.

Design Agency: *Meat and Potatoes, Inc.* Production Date: *2008.* Creative Director: *TJ River / Todd Gallopo.* Art Director: *TJ River.* Designer: *TJ River / Bahia Lahoud.* Client: *Neil George Salon / Beverly Hills.* Photography: *Meat and Potatoes, Inc.* Nationality: *USA.*

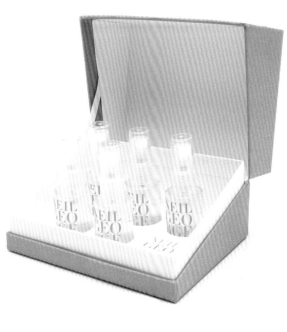

I.C.O.N.

I.C.O.N. has an extensive line of professional hair care products and has been quite successful thanks to their high quality products and progressive education programmes. Their image is high-end, fashion-forward and cutting-edge but their branding and visuals were falling short of their ever-rising standards. They recognised that a complete overhaul was in order if they were to achieve their goals and, having seen the work Version-X did with the Macadamia Natural Oil brand, they felt Version-X Design were perfectly suited for the task.

The designers started this intensive undertaking by addressing the overlying issue of organisation that was plaguing the line. The naming convention was reinvented. Products were categorised into two major groups: Care and Styling, each obviously different from the other. Care products are further grouped into families with colour coding that makes it easy to find other related products. To bring I.C.O.N.'s physical packaging into the 21st century the designers designed an all new custom bottle with embossed logo, contrasting soft touch and gloss elements and a modern yet timeless palette of white, greys and silver.

Design Agency: *Version–X Design*. Production Date: *2010*. Creative Director: *Chris Fasan*. Designer: *Chris Fasan / Adam Stoddard*. Client: *I.C.O.N.* Nationality: *USA*.

 Silk & Cotton

Branding Silk & Cotton, defining a new visual language, concept, logo, and packaging.

Designer Agency: *Dan Alexander & Co.* Production Date: *2008.* Designer: *Dan Alexander.* Client: *Silk & Cotton.* Nationality: *Serbia.*

12 Benefits

12 Benefits is a leading hair treatment formulated to maintain balance and reverse damage. Liska + Associates designed the logo and packaging to represent the twelve ways the product keeps hair healthy, shiny, and strong all day long.

Design Agency: *Liska+Associates.* Production Date: *2011.* Creative Director: *Steve Liska.* Designer: *Michael Brown.* Client: *Paulmaier Enterprises.* Nationality: *USA.*

 Prism – A Concentrated Hair Colour Pigment for Professional Use

Prism hair colour pigment concentrates revolutionise the way you dye your hair. The ability of a prism to break light into its constituent spectral colours serves as a metaphor that perfectly demonstrates endless possibilities the product offers. Every element of the packaging reflects the same simple and elegant theme.

Designer Agency: *Bob Helsinki*. Production Date: *2010*. Creative Director: *Ulla Lesevic*. Designer: *Ulla Lesevic*. Client: *Miraculos*. Nationality: *Finland*.

KC Professional –
Four Reasons
Take Away Colour

Take Away Colour is a permanent hair dye sold in hair salons for home use. Its mission is to remind you that dying your hair should be fun and experimental. The packaging overflows with attitude and personality that entice you to take a closer look at the product.

Design Agency: *Bob Helsinki*. Production Date: *2010*. Creative Director: *Ulla Lesevic*. Designer: *Ulla Lesevic*. Client: *Miraculos*. Nationality: *Finland*.

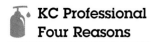

KC Professional
Four Reasons

Four Reasons is a professional hair care product range
sold in hair salons. The cheery design creates an
image that clearly distinguishes the products from the
competition and compels the customer to take a closer
look.

Designer Agency: *Bob Helsinki*. Production Date:
2010. Creative Director: *Ulla Lesevic*. Designer: *Ulla
Lesevic*. Client: *Miraculos*. Nationality: *Finland*.

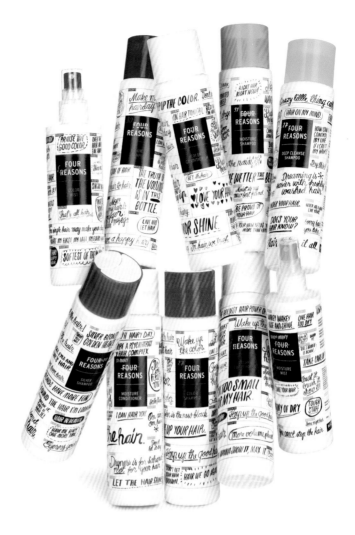

Haircare Xpressions

The object of this project was to utilise the container shapes of the Brand Haircare to create a new product line for young adults. For this, the theme "Xpressions" is aimed at inviting the consumer to experience something new. The typography interacts with the pack, giving a modern and unique style that ties the product line together. A subtle alteration in the type, that changes according to the composition of the phrases, creates a major visual impact and helps to associate with the personality of the brand. The shapes and images form hair styles mixed with the facial expressions of people and depict the product purpose. The idea is to print these images on matte metallic containers.

Design Agency: *Gworkshop*. Production Date: *2010*. Creative Director: *José Luis García Eguiguren*. Designer: *José Luis García Eguiguren*. Client: *Haircare*. Nationality: *Ecuador*.

 Lybar – Hair Spray

This was a study for the redesign of a traditional Czech hair spray. The brand was
not well perceived by consumers. The redesign was supposed to build a new image
of the gentleness of the natural based product, which helps your hair instead of
damaging it. It was also essential to build a clear product structure based on
product strength.

The illustration of each natural element was meant to express the strength and
carful approach of the product to consumers hair.

 Design Agency: *Butterflies & Hurricanes.* Production Date: *2010.* Designer:
Michaela Thomas. Client: *Lybar a.s.* Photography: *Viktor Tucek.* Nationality: *The
Czech Republic.*

Sturmayr Beauty Concept

Sturmayr Beauty Concept offers a highly sophisticated range of products each designed to help your hair stay fresh and healthy. The package shows a reduced and modern approach that wisely reflects the products proposition. It's clear and clean!

The shampoo bottle offers a reduced and modern design approach. Its glossy white surface combined with the fluorescent stripe embodies attributes that totally concur with the Sturmayr brand.

The small form factor package offers a smooth combination of simplicity and style. The unique flipcover gives a fresh approach to a classic container. The pump bottle with its slim design features a new mechanism for the spray handle. The fluorescent semitransparent stripe and it's glossy finish sticks to the product range.

Design Agency: *LOA Design Studio*. Production Date: *2010*. Creative Director: *Lucas Triebl / Stefan Fleig*. Designer: *Lucas Triebl*. Client: *Coiffeur Sturmayr GmbH*. Photography: *LOA Design Studio*. Nationality: *Austria*.

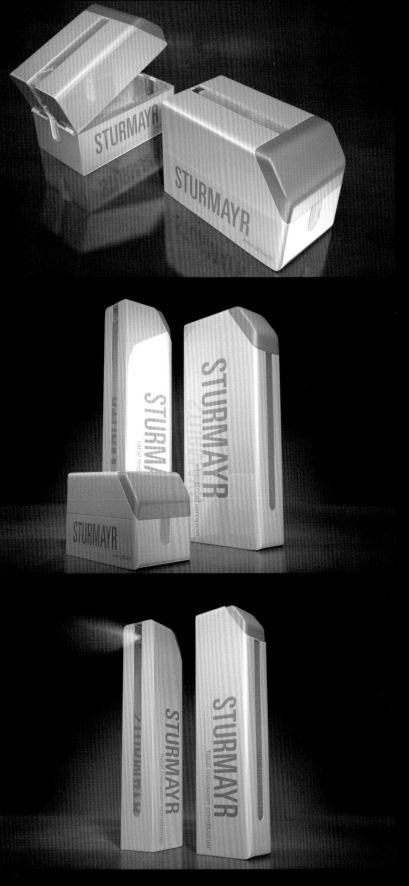

 Sturmayr Organics Haircare

Being the lead agency of Sturmayr Coiffeure for many years now, this is one of LOA's latest packaging design projects for the new Organics Haircare line of products. It's a good example for (cost) effective packaging design using standard form factors.

Designer Agency: *LOA Design Studio*. Production Date: *2010.* Creative Director: *Lucas Triebl / Stefan Fleig*. Designer: *Lucas Triebl*. Client: *Coiffeur Sturmayr GmbH*. Photography: *LOA Design Studio*. Nationality: *Austria*.

 Fred Segal Hair Care

For this 18-piece line of hair care products, a spin-off from the Fred Segal department store, Base used the brand's red and blue swirled stripes as a spring board to develop a set of similar stripe patterns, one for each package. In this way, Base questions the logic that logo marks today are the only way to identify a brand. Though the line was never produced, Base handled the design of all packaging, collaborating with Zorbit who was responsible for product engineering and, should the line have continued, production. With Zorbit, Base sourced matte white bottles, jars and tubes, and printed the individual striped patterns in high gloss, creating a juxtaposition between the two. All practical information including the logo, product information, and ingredients were placed on the back.

Design Agency: *Basedesign*. Production Date: *2007*. Client: *Fred Segal Beauty*. Nationality: *Spain*.

LUMINOSITY   ORANGETHERAPY   CHOCOLATETHERAPY   WINETHERAPY

SHAMPOO
AZIONE LUMINOSITÀ
PER CAPELLI SPENTI
E OPACHI

LUMINOSITY   ORANGETHERAPY   CHOCOLATETHERAPY   WINETHERAPY

SHAMPOO
AZIONE LUMINOSITÀ
PER CAPELLI SPENTI
E OPACHI

 Light Defense

Packaging for natural health hair products.

Design Agency: *Trelink*. Production Date: *2008*. Creative Director: *Manuel dall'Olio*. Nationality: *Italy*.

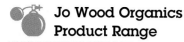

Jo Wood Organics
Product Range

Branding and packaging design for a massive range of skincare products, combining contrasting values of authentic organic and glamorous rock'n'roll.

Aloof created a cleaner and more distinct logo to better communicate the products' benefits. Subsequently, the designers refined the design of the luxury range, extended the range with new products, designed an e-commerce website and a supporting e-shot campaign.

Brand strategy, naming, brand identity, corporate identity, logo design, graphic design, packaging design, promotional literature, photography art direction, copywriting, e-commerce website design, brand guardianship, production management.

Design Agency: *Aloof*. Production Date: *2008*. Creative Director: Sam Aloof. Designer: *Jon Hodkinson / Andrew Scrase*. Client: *Jo Wood Organics*. Photography: *Leigh Simpson*. Nationality: *UK*.

Von Eusersdorff

The focus of the small fragrance label Von Eusersdorff is a commitment to authenticity. The design brings back the flower as the traditional ornament for fragrances, and goes back in history by drawing attention on the name of the label founder's ancestors. A skilled family of German emigrants who use to run an apothecary for nearly three centuries. The artisanal world of oils, herbs, spices and petals being the initial cradle of the perfume industry as people currently know it. The simple yet meticulous character of the packaging demonstrates that an understated end result still can look rich and sophisticated.

Design Agency: *Boy Bastiaens.* Production Date: *2010.* Art Director: *Boy Bastiaens.*
Designer: *Boy Bastiaens.* Client: *Von Eusersdorff.* Photography: *Boy Bastiaens.*
Nationality: *the Netherlands.*

VON EUSERSDORFF
NEW YORK

INSPIRINGLY DIFFERENT FRAGRANCES

ingredients
alcohol denat - water (aqua/eau) - fragrance (parfum)
benzyl benzoate - benzyl alcohol - limonene - linalool
coumarin - bht - ci14700 (fd&c red n°4)
ci19140 (fd&c yellow n°5) - ci42090 (fd&c blue n°1)
MADE IN FRANCE

P.O.BOX 11 NEW YORK N.Y. 10116-0011
www.voneusersdorff.com

100 ml   3.4 fl.oz

FOR EXTERNAL USE ONLY
POUR USAGE EXTERNE SEULEMENT   80%
                                      vol.   36M

VON EUSERSDORFF
NEW YORK

CLASSIC PATCHOULI
EAU DE PARFUM
100 ml

Sucrerie Parfum

Sucrerie is sensuality, glamour and charming.
Retrieving the classical language sensibility, the designers also rescued the Arts and Crafts / Art Nouveau aesthetic. They worked the illustration gesture, the appropriation and combination of typographies, the classical and subtle work space occupation and the elements' accuracy. Finally, the designers proposed a metallic label energizing the product identity and a packaging that invites to discover the perfume.

The fragrance was born in association with its name, which, as the translation indicates, is related with the candy's world sweetness, the bonbons' sent and the exquisitnes of caramel.

Design Agency: *WeikUp*. Production Date: *2009*. Creative Director: *Valeria Luchansky / Analía Fernandez Mollica / Flavio Siganda*. Designer: *Analía Fernandez Mollica*. Client: *Sucrerie*. Photography: *Flavio Siganda*. Nationality: *Argentina*.

S&G Fragrances

Soap & Glory is known for good value but has all of the perks of a higher end brand visually. This thinking needed to be applied to the fragrance designs. The two Soap & Glory fragrances need to compete amongst all of the high end/lifestyle brands on the market.

Launched in August 2009, Eau de Soap & Glory (Formula 2), is a glamorous, sexy fragrance perfect for day or night. The look is feminine, chic and timeless, with many vintage touches that all S&G products are known for. Formula 1, launching in 2011, has a modern daytime look complete with a summery fresh citrus style fragrance. The design is more stripped down yet is still undeniably part of the Soap & Glory family.

Design Agency: *Biggs&Co.* Production Date: *2008– 2009.* Designer: *Alli Truch / Kim Biggs.* Client: *Soap & Glory Cosmetics.* Photography: *Gavin Jones.* Nationality: *USA.*

Design of the bottle and graphics for men's fragrance. Codizia Man is a men's fragrance from the same brand which was launched three years ago the woman's market. It shares the quality product positioning, differential, and has a much lower price than high-end colognes. The packaging communicates similar attributes: sensuality, elegance, dynamism, etc. It does this following the same language and some of the characteristics of its female predecessor, as in the solution for the join between body and cap, but with changes that reaffirm their male personality: the colours and the volume, which moves from the horizontal to a vertical position for Codizia Man. It is also distributed exclusively in the Mercadona chain of supermarkets.

Design Agency: *Lavernia & Cienfuegos*. Production Date: *2010*. Designer: *Lavernia & Cienfuegos*. Client: *RNB Laboratories*. Nationality: *Spain*.

Codizia

Design of the bottle and graphics for women's fragrance.

Codizia is a fragrance developed for women who look for a quality and premium product, but at a much lower price than the top range perfumes. Its bottle tries to transmit these attributes: elegance, personality, sophistication... With its rounded shapes, the golden finished glasses, and the two curved white surfaces, which face each other, produce a light and reflection effect. The package has a graphic design that refers to the shapes and colours of the bottle. It is distributed exclusively at Mercadona shops.

Award: The Dieline Award, 2010

Design Agency: *Lavernia & Cienfuegos.* Production Date: *2007* Designer: *Lavernia & Cienfuegos.* Client: *RNB Laboratories.* Nationality: *Spain.*

Comotu

It is the design of the bottle and graphics for fragrances.

The collection of mass-market fragrances Comotu, designed for Mercadona, was aimed to be a simple product, in harmony with its price, but with a surprising presentation. In order to achieve a good brand image and minimise the costs of production, only one bottle design was used for the eight different fragrances, four in black for men and four in white for women. The distinct fragrances can be differentiated thanks to the different colours of their tops.

The shape of the bottle is rounded and curved, and the packages show shiny and metallic colours. The final design both of the bottle and its package has the gift to transmit high quality and modernity at a competitive price. It proves that a massmarket product with a good design can be very successful.

Design Agency: *Lavernia & Cienfuegos.* Production Date: *2005.* Designer: *Lavernia & Cienfuegos.* Client: *RNB Laboratories.* Nationality: *Spain.*

Comotu Amor

It is the design of the bottle and graphics for fragrances.

Comotu is a collection of fragrances designed for RNB, which can be found at Mercadona stores nationwide. It is a mass-market product that has a reduced price. The final design of the bottle and package transmits the idea of high quality and modernity at a competitive price. It proves that a mass-market product that has a good design can be very successful.

Design Agency: *Lavernia & Cienfuegos.* Production Date: *2005.* Designer: *Lavernia & Cienfuegos.* Client: *RNB Laboratories.* Nationality: *Spain.*

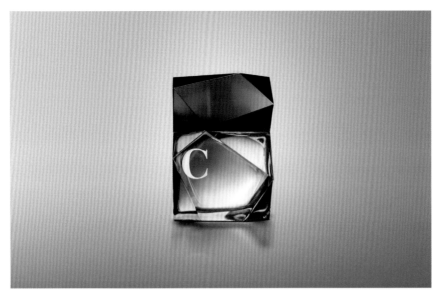

Criterio

It is the design of bottle and graphics for men's fragrance.

Criterio is a fragrance targeted at men searching for an exclusive product of quality, but at a lower price than perfumes of luxury range. The container suggests masculine elegance. It is a glass transparent polyhedron with edges and planes producing shines and reflections, helping to create a double sensation of hardness on one side and luxury on the other.

The packaging was solved with graphics that make reference to the faceted shape of the container. It is exclusively distributed at Mercadona.

Design Agency: *Lavernia & Cienfuegos*. Production Date: *2008*. Designer: *Lavernia & Cienfuegos*. Client: *RNB Laboratories*. Nationality: *Spain*.

Sisi Parfumerie & Cosmetiques

The project was a perfume store. At the centre of this project lies a texture-rich use of typography, highlighting the elegance and class associated with this trademark. The envelopes have been embossed with simple shapes and a catchword.

Design Agency: *Julien de Repentigny / Visual Advice*. Production Date: *2008*. Creative Director: *Julien de Repentigny*. Designer: *Julien de Repentigny*. Client: *Sisi Parfumerie & Cosmétiques*. Photography: *Julien de Repentigny*. Nationality: *Canada*.

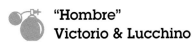

First masculine perfume of the Spanish stylists Victorio & Lucchino. "Hombre" is an iconic bottle shaped into a baroque pocket watch, for a sophisticated man and seducer.

Sotano Studio designed the bottle, the graphics, the packaging and the points of sale.

Design Agency: *Sotano Studio*. Production Date: *2009*. Creative Director: *Fanny le Bonniec*. Designer: *Oscar del Cerro*. Client: *Antonio Puig, S.A.* Photography: *Víctor Cucalón / Sotano Studio / Nin Studio*. Nationality: *Spain*.

"De Mil Colores" Rosario Flores

Translating the energy and the personality of the Spanish singer in a perfume, Sotano Studio created this ethnic and mysterious bottle. The graphics and the packaging are inspired by mandalas, magical talismans.

Design Agency: *Sotano Studio.* Production Date: *2010.* Creative Director: *Oscar del Cerro.* Designer: *Fanny le Bonniec.* Client: *Antonio Puig, S.A.* Photography: *Foto Combert.* Nationality: *Spain.*

 Concepts

Proposals developed during various projects for famous brands. Each design reflects the brand values and communicates a strong concept: the movement of curling and swirling ribbons, the whirling of a dancing dress or the tinkling of bracelets...

Design Agency: *Sotano Studio*. Production Date: *2008–2010*. Designer: *Fanny le Bonniec / Oscar del Cerro*. Photography: *Sotano Studio*. Nationality: *France / Spain*.

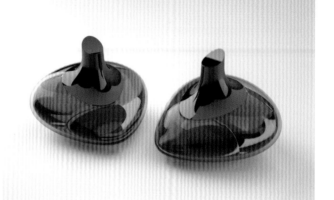

Montesinos

It is the design of bottle for women's fragrance.
A black glass cylinder wrapped in fuchsia in order
to evoke the creative world of Francis Montesinos
in which the traditional and the modern, the
Mediterranean and the sophisticated are combined.

Design Agency: *Lavernia & Cienfuegos*. Production
Date: *2008*. Designer: *Lavernia & Cienfuegos*. Client:
RNB Laboratories. Nationality: *Spain*.

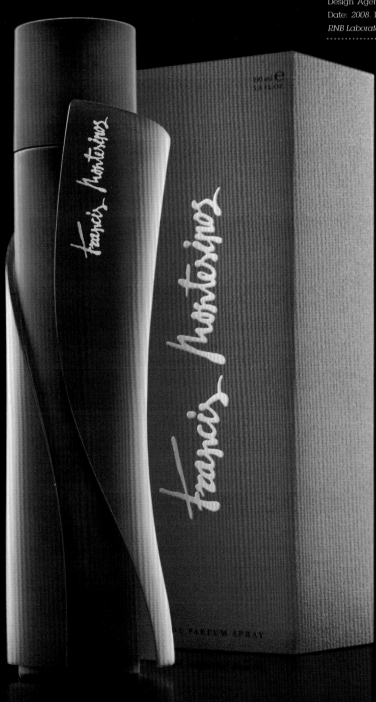

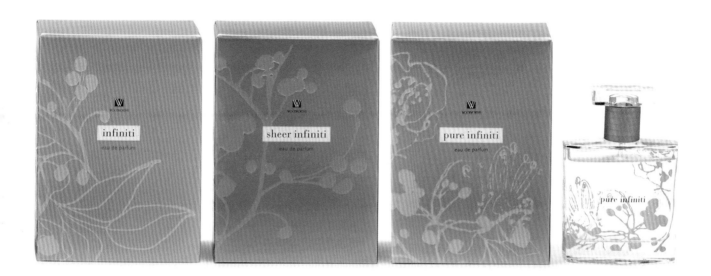

 Infiniti Fragrances Range

When designing the packaging for Woolworths' private label top tier fragrances, innovative stand-out on shelf was of utmost importance. Infiniti, Sheer Infiniti and Pure Infiniti were designed using simple typography and a single organic illustration which was cropped individually for each fragrance.

Luxurious cartons were printed using soft metallic inks, spot gloss UV varnish, overall matt laminated and embossed.

The bottles were printed with the name on the front, while the organic image reflects through the liquid from the back of the bottle.

Design Agency: *Moag Bailie Design Consultants*. Creative Director: *Annie Moag*. Nationality: *South Africa*.

Dizen

La Casa del Aroma is the ambient fragrances division from Sandra Marzzan. A flowered field is the image the designers create for the label.

Design Agency: *Dizen*. Production Date: *2006*. Creative Director: *Ignacio Eguiguren*. Designer: *Paula Menéndez*. Client: *Sandra Marzzan*. Photography: *Javier Izuel*. Nationality: *Argentina*.

Dizen

Tal Cual is the Eau de perfume of Sandra Marzzan. The packaging is feminine, with violet tones.

Design Agency: *Dizen*. Production Date: *2006*. Creative Director: *Ignacio Eguiguren*. Designer: *Paula Menéndez*. Client: *Sandra Marzzan*. Photography: *Javier Izuel*. Nationality: *Argentina*.

Minuit Prive

The object of this project was to develop a concept brand and a proposal for packaging as well as naming. It denotes elegance and exclusivity but is targeted towards a cost-conscious audience. The brief described the target audience as secure, elegant and sensual women with unique personality and style. The designers utilised the fragrance as the main element for the packaging as something exclusive with a connotation that the scent is something hidden, mysterious and secret. The designers chose names to encompass enchantment that they wanted to convey: "Minuit prive" (midnight), Desirée (Desired) Seduisante (Seductive) and Mysterieuse (Mysterious). The packaging also had to reflect the concepts: modern with a hint of classic appeal. The body of the bottle is reminiscent of the timeless perfumes while the encasing gives a more contemporary touch that links the concept of fluid movement depicted as smoke.

Production Date: *2010*. Creative Director: *José Luis García Eguiguren / Leonor Pinto / Cátia Caeiro*. Designer: *José Luis García Eguiguren / Leonor Pinto / Cátia Caeiro*. Client: *Helena Hess*. Nationality: *Spain*.

HELENA HESS
MINUIT PRIVÉ
MYSTERIEUSE

HELENA HESS
MINUIT PRIVÉ
DÉSIRE

HELENA HESS
MINUIT PRIVÉ

HELENA HESS
MINUIT PRIVÉ
DÉSIRE

HELENA HESS
MINUIT PRIVÉ

 21 Drops

The goal of the design was to achieve a contemporary sensibility while respecting the heritage of aromatherapy and the artisanal nature of the product. This was achieved through the amalgamation of a vibrant colour palette and font-driven numerical graphics combined with embossed patterns and a kraft substrate.

Design Agency: *Purpose–Built*. Production Date: *2010*. Creative Director: *Kelly Kovack*. Designer: *Mi Rae Park*. Client: *21 Drops*. Photography: *Raymond Hom / Paul Tillinghast*. Nationality: *USA*.

 ## Marc Jacobs Perfume Proposal

This was a proposal for a Marc Jacobs luxury fragrance. The 50 - millilitre - bottle has interchangeable caps connected with a gold chain similar to the hardware on Marc Jacobs handbags.

The 100 - millilitre has a detachable mini eau de toilette to take on the go.

Design Agency: *BUREAU–TM*. Creative Director: *Tommy Everett*. Client: *Coty Prestige*. Nationality: *USA*.

John Galliano First Fragrance
Bottling & Packaging

Vivacious and fashionable, John Galliano's first perfume was inspired by the
designer's muse, a mystical woman who's eccentric, contradictory, seductive and
sensual. While contemporary in look, the bottle pays tribute to the Belle Epoque.
The glass, pleated and pierced by the Poiret rose so dear to the designer, recalls the
gowns depicted in Boldini's paintings.

Design Agency: *Centdegres*. Production Date: *2008*. Creative Director: *Elie
Papiernik*. Client: *John Galliano*. Nationality: *France*.

 Lanvin Marry Me
Product Design & Packaging

Largely inspired by the world of Albert Elbaz, the bottle features the character of the
Lanvin fashion house. Feminine and modern, the bottle reinterprets the bow motif in
an original and offbeat way.

Design Agency: *Centdegres.* Production Date: *2010.* Creative Director: *Tommy
Everett.* Client: *LANVIN.* Photography: *Lanvin Parfums.* Nationality: *France.*

Pure Espoir Packaging Bottle and Flask Design

The inspiration came from the feather-light elements found in nature, the design capturing this infinite lightness. The bottle is as soft and delicate as a rose petal, seemingly ready to take off at any moment, lifted by a gentle breeze. The round form fits neatly into the palm of the hand, nestling there naturally.

Design Agency: *Centdegres.* Production Date: *2007.* Creative Director: *Elie Papiernik.* Client: *Amore Pacific.* Nationality: *France.*

The Body Shop International PLC is a natural and ethical beauty brand with over 2,500 stores worldwide. The Body Shop carries a wide range of products for the body, face, hair and home.

Sandra Planeta, the founder of Planeta Design worked with the Body Shop for many years as the head of the global packaging division. One of the greatest challenges was to handle the multi language labelling task. The Body Shop's products are sold in many different markets, each with their own legal directions that have to be satisfied. Customising the packaging for each market was impossible due to its inflexibility as well as the high costs. The result of the packaging was a communication solution that worked on all markets as well as being clear and attractive to the customer.

Sandra Planeta was instrumental in the re-vamping of the brand's packaging with clean graphic packaging, characterised by photographic elements of the main ingredients. Scent me, Invent Your Scent, Born Lippy, Men's fragrance and skincare, and haircare have all gone through Sandra's meticulous design process.

Design Agency: *Planeta Design*. Production Date: *2000–2005*. Creative Director: *Sandra Planeta*. Client: *The Body Shop International plc*. Photography: *Per Mäkitalo*. Nationality: *Sweden*.

 Freedom of Creation
Packaging for L'Oreal

On the occasion of the launch of its "Gold Future" eye reviver cream in 2006, Helena Rubinstein, a brand of L'Oreal, has asked Freedom of Creation to create an intriguing packaging, capable to express the preciousness of the product containing Micro-Active Gold.

Inspired by the fluidity of the cream, Janne Kyttanen, founder of FOC and designer of the packaging, has developed an organic spherical envelope realised with flexible nylon through 3D printing. This gold-finished shell bares the original "Gold Future" cream packaging in a sensual way, unwrapping it in a soft, spiral movement.

Freedom of Creation designed and produced a limited edition of 66 pieces of this unique Helena Rubinstein "Gold Future" packaging.

Design Agency: *Freedom of Creation*. Production Date: *2006*. Designer: *Janne Kyttanen*. Nationality: *The Netherlands*.

Maura & Richard

Wedding Invitation and Bridal Favors. Black magic roses, and hints of luxurious mother of pearl, were used as inspiration. The vintage pattern and type treatment, allowed this lovely assortment to fit perfectly in a romantic fall setting.

Design Agency: *Coterie New York.* Production Date: *2009.* Designer: *Erika Nielsen.* Client: *Maura Alexander.* Photography: *Paul Tillinghast.* Nationality: *USA.*

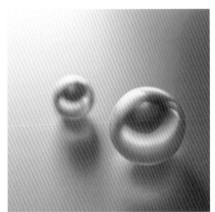

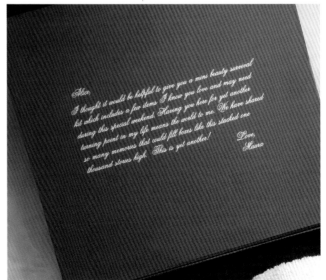

Daniele de Winter

Packaging Design in cooperation with Benjamin Ehrhardt.

The brand De Winter implies scientific research, natural ingredients and a high society luxury brand. The designers tried to keep the packaging of the cosmetics very clean and reduced. This should underline the exclusive character of the brand. A simple cylinder with one degree of bevel. This makes the product special without obvious "styling". The bottom part of the product is made of glass. This shows the background of the scientific research and stands for honesty and highest quality of the ingredients. It's a matter of cause or self-evident that this product is 100% natural and the best for your body.

Design Agency: *AdbK Stuttgart.* Production Date: *2008.* Designer: *Gerhardt Kellermann / Benjamin Ehrhardt.* Client: *Autrepart Nature.* Nationality: *Germany.*

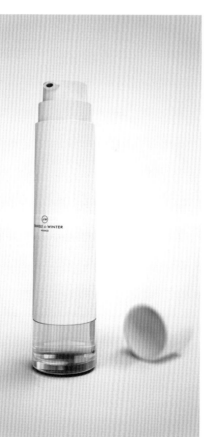

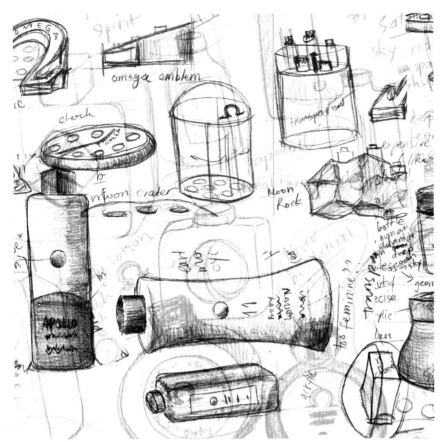

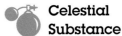 # Celestial Substance

To create a line of skin care products for an existing brand that is far removed from the world of cosmetics. By understanding the company's background, brand equity, and image, the goal is to create compelling packaging for retail markets and cohesive product extensions with an in-store display.

Production Date: *2010.* Designer: *Tran Huynh.* Client: *Academy of Art University, School of Graphic Design, San Francisco.* Nationality: *USA.*

Green People—Packaging Design
—Oy!

Oy! – Organic Young! burst* named and designed a teen range of skin care products for Green People. The language of the packs communicates to the teenagers.

Design Agency: *burst**. Production Date: *2008*. Creative Director: *Kasia Rust*. Designer: *Sophie Mockford*. Client: *Green People*. Nationality: *UK*.

IDC

Mookai was mandated to re-package and create a campaign for a new anti aging skincare line which uniquely targets 16 main causes of skin aging. The designers developed the REGEN 16 name and icon to call attention to this unique proposition. The name IDC and icon were the starting point. From there the designers researched vessel shapes, colours, fonts and created key text to communicate the product benefits. They wanted to give the product a clinical and pure esthetic. The product was launched in France in the Parashop drugstore chain and a year later came into the Canadian and International markets.

Design Agency: *Mookai Communications*. Production Date: *2010*. Creative Director: *Lori von Sychowski*. Art Director: *Lori von Sychowski*. Designer: *Stefanie Sosiak*. Client: *Immanence IDC*. Photography: *Carlo Hindian*. Nationality: *Canada*.

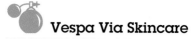

Vespa Via Skincare

The internationally iconic Vespa carries a rich heritage and is a perfect candidate for a new skincare line. Highlighting the brand in a fresh and bold way, Vespa Via is an imagined concept behind a complete line of unisex products designed to fit the contemporary lifestyle.

Production Date: *2010.* Designer: *Jenny Pan.* Client: *Academic.* Photography: *Rob Villanueva.* Nationality: *USA.*

 Kiehl's Creme de Corp

The design agency, ilovedust, continuing their great relationship with Kiehl's, worked with them to create a range of bespoke illustrated labels. The idea behind this, was to enable the labels to be personalised to carry individual messages to friends and family or indeed any recipient of this great product! Customers can type in their messages when visiting Kiehl's Store in New York and the labels are printed and applied to bottles of Kiehl's famous Creme de Corps.

Design Agency: *ilovedust*. Production Date: *2010*. Designer: *ilovedust*. Client: *Kiehl's*. Photography: *ilovedust*. Nationality: *UK*.

One Love Organics
Skincare Packaging

This product line is about artisanal quality and simplicity. The entire line is composed of just four products, each of which is highly concentrated and multi-functional. Three of the products are made by hand and the 4th is made in small batches exclusively for One Love Organics. The designers carried this idea of hand - crafted simple beauty throughout the packaging. Simplicity is expressed through form (with minimal packaging components) and hand - crafted quality is suggested through the label design (with hand - drawn elements and a whimsical brand voice). The designers used minimal packaging and put in depth educational information on the website instead of on a box or interior pamphlet.

Hand written product names suggest the personal, hand - crafted quality of the products. While the hand drawn patterns subtly suggest the action of each product. Whimsical names and humorous descriptions bring a unique voice to the brand and reflect the belief that happiness is the foundation of true beauty.

Design Agency: *One Love Organics*. Production Date: *2010*. Creative Director: *Kendra Inman*. Designer: *Kendra Inman*. Client: *One Love Organics*. Photography: *Scott Clark*. Nationality: *USA*.

Little Me Organics

This is a re-brand from the ground up for a popular a range of organic baby toiletries made from organic ingredients that contain gentle formulations and avoid synthetic fragrances. This will be found in over 300 stores across the England.

The brief was to re-design the packs to appeal to mothers and to stand out in an extremely competitive market place, whilst communicating the Organic benefits and origins of the product. The designers achieved this by using a largely decorative floral illustration incorporating the brand identity with the use of bold, bright colours, which emulate children's book illustrations.

Design Agency: *R Design*. Production Date: *2008*. Creative Director: *Dave Richmond*. Designer: *Charlotte Hayes*. Client: *KMI Brands*. Nationality: *UK*.

Micheline Arcier Aromatherapie

The brand had become jaded and outdated through lack of design and marketing
initiative.

R Design developed the new brand identity which was incorporated across
packaging, Knightsbridge Clinic, and website as part of total brand update.
Particular attention was paid to retaining the integrity, authority and quality nature
of the brand. This was achieved through an individual logo redesign with better
impact and vibrant and distinctive colour used to produce beautiful packaging of
great quality sympathetic with the brand's heritage yet relevant and contemporary.

Design Agency: *R Design*. Production Date: *2006*. Creative Director: *Dave
Richmond*. Designer: *Charlotte Hayes*. Client: *Micheline Arcier Aromatherapie*.
Nationality: *UK*.

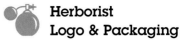

Herborist
Logo & Packaging

Herborist is a premium cosmetics brand inspired from the ancestral traditions of traditional Chinese Medicine. The objective was to give Herborist a more contemporary, international look by updating the logo and creating a more distinctive range. The design style is inspired from bamboo, a detail that gives a touch of nature and refinement. It conveys the knowhow and the diversity and also the harmony through the circle.

Design Agency: *Centdegres.* Production Date: *2009.* Creative Director: *Elie Papiernik.* Client: *JAHWA.* Nationality: *France.*

Major

Packaging for thermal beauty/wellness products.

Design Agency: *Trelink*. Production Date: *2009*.
Creative Director: *Manuel dall'Olio*. Nationality: *Italy*.

 **Givenchy Eaudemoiselle
Bottling & Packaging**

Givenchy wanted to create an eau de toilette that captured the brand's essence,
with an identity of its own reflecting the substance of a perfume and setting it apart
from the category's familiar offerings.

Design Agency: *Centdegres*. Production Date: *2010*. Creative Director: *Elie
Papiernik*. Client: *Givenchy*. Photography: *Boris Ovini / Parfums Givenchy*.
Nationality: *France*.

Odin Fragrance

The Odin fragrance series represents a joint venture and creative collaboration between Odin and Purpose-Built. The packaging is an exploration in black with contrasting materials and surfaced to promote discovery and a tactile experience.

Design Agency: *Purpose–Built*. Production Date: *2009*. Creative Director: *Larry Paul / Eddy Chai*. Designer: *Emily Kim*. Client: *Odin*. Nationality: *USA*.

Index

©2010 by Design Media Publishing Limited
This edition published in February 2012

Design Media Publishing Limited
20/F Manulife Tower
169 Electric Rd, North Point
Hong Kong
Tel: 00852-28672587
Fax: 00852-25050411
E-mail: Kevinchoy@designmediahk.com
www.designmediahk.com

Documentation: Jie ZHOU, Liying WANG, Muzi
            GUAN, Haoyang LU, Lin LIN
Proofreading: Qian YIN
Design/Layout: Lin LIN

ISBN 978-988-15071-7-4

Printed in China